Digital Photography

Before & After Makeovers™

WILEY

Wiley Publishing, Inc.

By Julie Adair King

Digital Photography Before & After Makeovers™

Published by
Wiley Publishing, Inc.
111 River Street
Hoboken, NJ 07030-5774
www.wiley.com

Copyright © 2006 by Wiley Publishing, Inc., Indianapolis, Indiana

Published by Wiley Publishing, Inc., Indianapolis, Indiana

Published simultaneously in Canada

For general information on our other products and services, please contact our Customer Care Department within the U.S. at 800-762-2974, outside the U.S. at 317-572-3993, or fax 317-572-4002.

For technical support, please visit www.wiley.com/techsupport.

Wiley also publishes its books in a variety of electronic formats. Some content that appears in print may not be available in electronic books.

Library of Congress Control Number: 2006927761

ISBN-13: 978-0-471-76116-7

ISBN-10: 0-471-76116-8

Manufactured in the United States of America

10 9 8 7 6 5 4 3 2 1

1K/RZ/QX/QW/IN

WILEY

Meet the Author

Courtesy Heidi Mielke

Julie Adair King is the author of many books about digital photography and imaging. Her most recent titles include *Digital Photography For Dummies, Shoot Like a Pro!: Digital Photography Techniques, Julie King's Everyday Photoshop for Photographers,* and *Julie King's Everyday Photoshop Elements.* Other works include *Photo Retouching & Restoration For Dummies, Adobe PhotoDeluxe For Dummies, Adobe PhotoDeluxe 4.0 For Dummies,* and *Microsoft PhotoDraw 2000 For Dummies.* A graduate of Purdue University, King resides in Indianapolis, Indiana.

Dedication

This book is dedicated to my parents, Dale and Barbara King. Thank you for trusting me enough to never ask when I am going to get a "real job" and for the support that helps me to be successful at this one. I love you and am inspired by you always.

Author's Acknowledgments

This book would not have been possible without the hard work and creative talent of the editorial and production teams at John Wiley & Sons, Inc., starting with the always supportive and unflappable editor Kim Darosett. Kim, thank you for your great editorial insights as well as for talking me down during my not infrequent moments of panic. Thanks also to copy editor Virginia Sanders and to Steve Hayes, Paul Levesque, Leah Cameron, Mary Bednarek, and the rest of the *Before & After Makeovers* editorial crew. I am grateful as well for the efforts of the design and production team, led by project coordinator Erin Smith.

In addition, I am deeply indebted to technical editor, Alfred DeBat, for being so willing to lend his years of knowledge and experience to this project. Al, you have saved me from many an embarrassing blooper, and I can never thank you enough.

More big hugs go to Annabelle Wallnau, for shooting the Chapter 2 sunset portraits of Tamara, and to all the people who so patiently posed for me, including Adam, April (finally got you to agree!), Betsy, Dylan, Evan, Lana, Lisa, Newton, Paige, Sam, Simone, and Tatiana. The very best part of writing this book was getting to spend time with all of you.

Finally, I am forever blessed by the support of my family and friends, without whom nothing would mean anything. Thank you for allowing me to be my ridiculous self and only rolling your eyes at me occasionally, when surely I deserve it on a daily basis.

Publisher's Acknowledgments

We're proud of this book; please send us your comments through at www.wiley.com/.

Some of the people who helped bring this book to market include the following:

Acquisitions, Editorial, and Media Development

Project Editor: **Kim Darosett**

Acquisitions Editor: **Steve Hayes**

Copy Editor: **Virginia Sanders**

Technical Editor: **Alfred DeBat**

Editorial Manager: **Leah Cameron**

Media Development Manager: **Laura VanWinkle**

Editorial Assistant: **Amanda Foxworth**

Sr. Editorial Assistant: **Cherie Case**

Composition Services

Project Coordinator: **Erin Smith**

Book Designer: **LeAndra Hosier**

Layout and Graphics: **Jennifer Click, Stephanie D. Jumper, Lynsey Osborn, Ron Terry**

Proofreaders: **Vicki Broyles, Jessica Kramer, Jennifer Stanley**

Indexer: **Julie Kawabata**

Cover Design: **Daniela Richardson**

Publishing and Editorial for Technology Dummies

Richard Swadley, Vice President and Executive Group Publisher

Andy Cummings, Vice President and Publisher

Mary Bednarek, Executive Acquisitions Director

Mary C. Corder, Editorial Director

Publishing for Consumer Dummies

Diane Graves Steele, Vice President and Publisher

Joyce Pepple, Acquisitions Director

Composition Services

Gerry Fahey, Vice President of Production Services

Debbie Stailey, Director of Composition Services

Table of Contents

Introduction   1

1 SETTING UP YOUR CAMERA AND DIGITAL DARKROOM   6

Turn Down ISO to Stifle Noise   8

Capture More Pixels for Better Prints   10

Bury JPEG Artifacts   14

Go Raw for Maximum Quality and Control   16

Turn Off Digital Zoom   23

Expand Your Palette with a Wider-Gamut Color Space   24

Frame Loosely for Greater Print Flexibility   26

Profile Your Monitor for Accurate Image Display   28

Make Friends with Your Photo Editor   30

Customize Your Tool Brush to the Job   32

Choose Your Paint Colors   36

Master the Art of Selecting   38

Wave the Magic Wand to Select by Color   43

2 EXPOSURE AND LIGHTING MAKEOVERS   46

Exposing a Better Picture   48

Autoexposure Hack #1: Change the Metering Mode   52

Autoexposure Hack #2: EV Compensation   54

Go Flash Free for Better Indoor Portraits   56

Use Fill Flash to Improve Outdoor Portraits   60

Snap a More Colorful Sunset Portrait   62

Banish Reflections and Shadows from Product Shots   64

Correct Exposure in Your Photo Editor   69

Reveal Lost Shadow Detail   73

3 FOCUS MAKEOVERS — 76

Draw Attention to Your Subject with Focus — 78

Blur a Busy Background in Your Photo Editor — 83

Steady the Camera, Sharpen the Shot — 86

Solve Autofocus Miscues — 89

Bring More of the Scene into Focus — 94

Increase Shutter Speed to Freeze Action — 96

Turn Water into Mist with a Slow Shutter — 98

Discover Drama in the Details with Macro-Focusing Power — 100

Create the Illusion of Sharper Focus — 102

4 COLOR MAKEOVERS — 108

Neutralize Light with Manual White Balancing — 110

Add Warmth for Better Portraits — 112

Tweak Color Balance in Your Photo Editor — 114

Remove a Color Cast with a Single Click — 117

Dial Back Saturation to Reveal Subtle Details — 118

Direct the Eye with Color — 120

Lower the Odds of Red Eye — 122

Repair Red Eye (Or Green, Yellow, or White Eye) — 124

Add Impact by Going Gray — 127

Give Your Picture an Antique Look — 129

5 MORE DIGITAL DARKROOM MAKEOVERS — 132

Straighten a Tilting Image — 134

Straighten Converging Verticals — 136

Crop to a Better Composition — 139

Crop to Specific Dimensions — 142

Clone Away Intrusive Objects — 144

Apply a Blur to Diminish Noise — 150

Make a High-Resolution Image Web Friendly — 153

6 EXTREME MAKEOVERS 158

Turn Sorry Snapshots into Framable Winners 160

Take a Low-Light Landscape from Dark and Drab to Bright and Fab 166

Turn a Blurry Mess into an Animal Adventure 170

Give Your Product Shots More Sales Appeal 177

APPENDIX: GLOSSARY AND QUICK REFERENCE GUIDE 182

Glossary of Digital Photography Terms 184

Picture Makeover Quick Reference 191

Symbol Quick Reference 193

Products/Services Quick Reference 194

My Camera Quick Reference 195

Set Up Color Management in Photoshop Elements 197

INDEX 203

Introduction

As someone who's been writing about digital photography for a long time, I'm often asked to explain the benefits of this new technology. The financial advantages are clear: You no longer have to pay for film, processing, and printing. Instead, you record pictures on memory cards that you can use repeatedly, and you pay only for the prints you really like. In my opinion, though, a more important benefit is the ability to instantly review images on the camera monitor. So whether you're taking pictures of a wedding, birthday party, vacation spot, or just your dog's new haircut, you no longer have to cross your fingers and hope that you got the shot you wanted. You know right away whether you captured a winner or need to try again.

Realizing that your picture has a problem, though, doesn't mean that you know what camera settings you should change to fix it. Looking for answers in your camera manual — if you can even find it — often leads only to more confusion. On top of all the traditional photography terms you encounter — *aperture, depth of field, focal length,* and so on — manuals are full of digital imaging and computing lingo, which is just as user unfriendly. And even if you can decipher the language, most manuals simply describe how to access a particular camera control, not how to choose the right combination of settings for the type of picture you want to take.

That's where *Digital Photography Before & After Makeovers* comes in. Using plain English and tons of illustrations, this book provides an easy-to-use troubleshooting guide to the most common digital photography problems. Is your subject underexposed, for example, even though the rest of the image looks fine? Do you get nothing but a blurry mess when you take pictures of your teen playing soccer? Whether you shoot with a top-of-the-line digital SLR or a basic point-and-shoot model, this book offers simple techniques to fix these and a host of other picture problems.

What Makes This Book Different?

Unlike most photography books, *Digital Photography Before & After Makeovers* doesn't make you wade through long paragraphs of explanatory text to get the answers you need. Instead, each chapter contains a series of fully illustrated makeovers that walk you step-by-step through the process of diagnosing and fixing specific picture problems.

In addition, for times when no combination of camera settings or photographic tricks produces the results you want, this book includes how-to's for fixing exposure, focus, color, and minor flaws in your photo editing program. Along the way, you can also find explanations of all those unfamiliar techie terms that may have you feeling like a digital photography outsider. (I know; I've been there!)

Here's a quick preview of the topics each chapter addresses.

Chapter 1: Setting Up Your Camera and Digital Darkroom

A big part of getting the best results from your digital camera is choosing the right initial picture-quality settings. Chapter 1 helps you set up your camera to produce high-quality images, discussing such critical settings as resolution, file format, color space, and ISO. The chapter concludes by introducing basic photo-editing tools and skills, such as customizing tool brushes and selecting the area of the picture you want to alter.

Chapter 2: Exposure and Lighting Makeovers

Look here for a variety of solutions you can use when your picture is too dark or too bright. In addition to explaining basic exposure controls — aperture, shutter speed, and ISO — Chapter 2 offers tricks that enable you to better control exposure even when your camera offers only fully automatic exposure. And as the chapter title promises, some makeovers feature lighting techniques that are very simple yet make big improvements in your portrait and still-life photos.

Chapter 3: Focus Makeovers

Having trouble getting your camera to focus correctly? Want to find out how the pros manipulate focus to produce more powerful images? Chapter 3 makeovers discuss all things focus-related, including how to create the illusion of sharper or softer focus in your photo editor.

Chapter 4: Color Makeovers

Whether you want your image colors to be bolder, less saturated, warmer, or cooler, Chapter 4 shows you how to get the job done. Among other topics, this chapter explains how to use your camera's white-balance control to add or remove a color cast and how to create a beautiful black-and-white or sepia-toned photo from a color original.

Chapter 5: More Digital Darkroom Makeovers

Chapters 2 through 4 all include a few makeovers that illustrate how to use simple photo-editing tools to achieve exposure, focus, or color changes that you can't get your camera to deliver. The makeovers in Chapter 5 feature photo-editing tricks that enable you to correct or alter other aspects of your pictures. Subjects covered include cropping your picture, removing small flaws, and straightening a tilting horizon line.

Chapter 6: Extreme Makeovers

You know those television shows that overhaul an entire room or even a whole house? The idea behind Chapter 6 is the same, although, regrettably, there are no dreamy carpenters to ogle. What you can study are makeovers that incorporate multiple techniques to completely transform a very ugly image into a frame-worthy photo.

Appendix: Glossary and Quick Reference Guide

I fully explain digital photography terms as I introduce them throughout the book. But if you need a refresher and don't want to go searching through the chapters to find the meaning of a particular phrase, just flip to the appendix, which contains a complete glossary. Following the glossary are four quick-reference charts. One provides a troubleshooting checklist; another decodes common camera-control symbols; and the third points you to the Web sites of manufacturers whose products and services are mentioned in the book. The fourth provides space for you to note which camera controls are available on your model and how to access them. Finally, for readers who use Photoshop Elements 4.0 (the photo software featured in some makeovers), the last part of the appendix explains how to set up that program to improve color consistency between on-screen images and printed photos.

A Few Final Notes about Using This Book

I'm a firm believer that introductions should be short, so I won't ramble on much further. However, I do need to share a few final bits of information about this book:

➤ **Suggested order of reading:** This book is written so that you can dive into any chapter, any makeover, in no particular order. However, if you're brand new to both photography and digital imaging, things will make more sense if you read Chapter 1 first. I also suggest that you explore the first few pages of both Chapter 2 and Chapter 3, which explain the basics of exposure and focus, respectively, before you move on to the other makeovers.

➤ **Camera types:** The majority of techniques in this book apply no matter what type of camera you use. Most makeover steps initially explain what settings to try if you use an advanced camera that offers a long list of capture options, including manual control over exposure and focus. Then,

I follow up with alternative methods that work with a more basic, point-and-shoot model.

➤ **Feature illustrations:** In some illustrations, you see camera dials, monitors, and symbols (such as a symbol indicating a specific flash setting or focus mode). These graphics are generic, created for this book, and not specific to any one camera. The controls and symbols on your camera may look slightly different, so you may want to keep your camera manual handy as a second reference as you read.

➤ **Photo-editing makeovers:** To provide specific photo-editing instructions, I had to select a particular program to feature. I opted for Adobe Photoshop Elements 4.0 because it is relatively inexpensive, is available for both Windows and Macintosh systems, and contains a nice selection of editing tools. However, if you use another version of that program or another program altogether, you should be able to easily translate the steps to your software.

Within the steps, you may see an instruction that reads something like "Choose Enhance➪ Adjust Color➪Adjust Hue/Saturation." The arrows indicate that you're looking at a chain of commands that you need to select from the program menus. In this case, for example, you would click the Enhance menu, click Adjust Color, and then click Adjust Hue/Saturation.

Finally, and perhaps most important, I want to stress that if you are new to either photography or digital imaging, or both, you may feel overwhelmed when you first explore this book. Believe me, that's completely natural. No matter how easy the camera commercials make digital photography seem, this stuff is complicated — doubly so if you're also a computer novice.

But hang in there and make it a point to practice just one technique each time you head out with your camera. Little by little, you'll build the skills you need to turn a disappointing Before shot into a terrific After. Even better, your new-found knowledge will soon become second nature, and you'll be able to skip the Before stage altogether, shooting beautiful images on the first try.

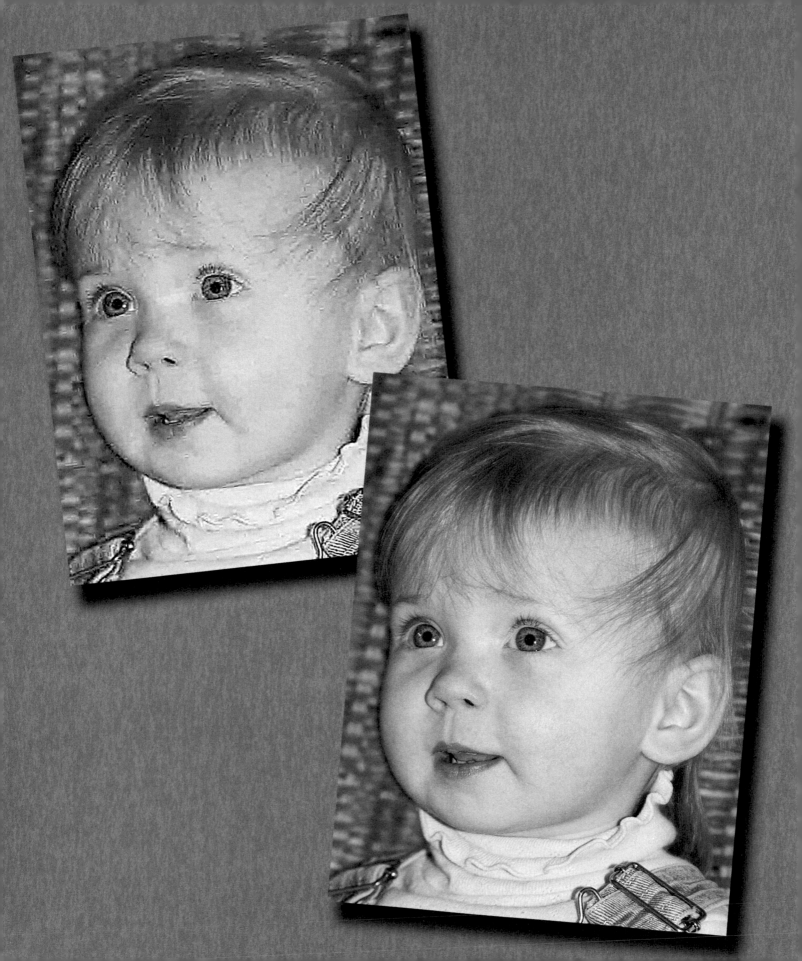

1

SETTING UP YOUR CAMERA AND DIGITAL DARKROOM

What makes a great picture? Strong composition? An interesting subject? Perfect focus, exposure, and color?

Without a doubt, all those factors are essential to a winning image. But they're meaningless unless you first set up your digital camera to produce the best picture quality.

When I speak of picture quality, I'm referring not to some artistic aesthetic, but to the technical rendering of the image — how "clean" the photo appears, if you will. Certain camera settings can cause a picture to look jagged or blocky, exhibit weird color halos here and there, be littered with random color speckles, or all of the above. A high-quality image is free of these defects.

So that the makeover techniques you discover in the rest of the book can really pay off, this chapter helps you set up your camera to produce the best picture quality. Look here for information about such critical subjects as resolution, file format, ISO, color space, and more. (If that entire sentence sounded like gibberish, don't worry; all is made clear in the pages to come.)

Of course, no matter what camera settings you use, you aren't going to turn out a perfect picture *every* time, which is why the makeover chapters include photo-retouching tricks as well as photographic tips. To get you started on the right foot in that department, this chapter also offers advice on setting up your digital darkroom as well as a primer on using the core retouching tools in Photoshop Elements 4.0, the software featured in this book. Read through this information even if you don't use Elements; the tools in your photo-editing program likely work much the same.

Turn Down ISO to Stifle Noise

Do you remember the last time you bought film? On the side of the box, you might have spotted an *ISO rating:* 200, 400, and 800 are the most common.

The ISO rating indicates the film's sensitivity to light — *film speed,* in photography lingo. ISO stands for International Organization for Standardization, the group that set the speed ratings.

Similarly, your digital camera offers an ISO control that enables you to adjust the camera's light sensitivity. If you raise the ISO value, you need less light to expose the image, which means that you can shoot in darker locations without adding flash. You also may be able to use a smaller aperture, faster shutter speed, or both. (Chapter 2 explains aperture and shutter speed.)

However, this added exposure latitude costs you in terms of picture quality. Raising the ISO setting often causes *noise,* a defect that makes your picture look as though it has been sprinkled with fine grains of sand. The higher the ISO, the greater the noise potential, as illustrated by the four turtle images taken at ISO 1600, 640, 400, and 200. (The same problem occurs with film, by the way.)

The amount of noise generated at each ISO setting varies from camera to camera, so take some test shots to find out how high you can go before picture quality becomes unacceptable.

Basic	Custom 1	Custom 2
Sensitivity	ISO 400	
Metering mode	ISO 200	
Exp. comp.	• ISO 100	
Noise reductn	Auto	
Auto reset		

ISO 1600

ISO 640

Of course, in very dim lighting, you simply may not be able to get the shot unless you raise the ISO setting. In that case, go ahead and capture the image at a couple of lower ISO settings, too. You may find that you get a better picture by applying your photo editor's exposure-adjustment filters to a too-dark image than you get by taking the shot at a very high ISO setting. (Chapter 2 introduces you to some of these filters.)

Also keep in mind that noise becomes more visible as you enlarge your photo, as illustrated here. In addition, the eye has an easier time detecting noise in areas that feature soft focus or flat colors, such as in the backgrounds of the turtle pictures. In highly detailed areas, such as around the turtle's eye, noise has more opportunity to hide.

Julie's Take: Finally, because the impact of ISO noise is so great, I recommend that you do not take advantage of the Auto ISO setting found on some cameras. In this mode, the camera increases ISO as it sees fit — and that's a decision that you, not the camera, should make.

If you do wind up with a noisy picture, you may be able to soften its impact by applying a blurring filter in your photo editor. Some programs even have dedicated noise-removal filters. See Chapter 5 for a look at your noise-removal options.

ISO 400

ISO 200

Capture More Pixels for Better Prints

Your digital camera likely offers two or more *resolution* settings. The resolution setting determines the number of pixels in the image. Pixels — short for *picture elements* — are the tiny squares of color from which digital photos are built.

How many pixels are enough? The answer depends on whether you want to print your photo or to use it for some on-screen purpose, such as in an online photo album or a multimedia presentation.

➤ **Printed photos:** For good prints, you need at least 200 pixels per inch, or 200 *ppi*. A 4 x 6-inch print, for example, requires 800 x 1200 pixels. (Note that ppi refers to pixels per *linear* inch, not square inch.) When a printed photo lacks adequate pixels, details are poorly rendered, and diagonal and curved lines appear jagged. Compare the low-resolution, 75-ppi lion image to the right with the 200-ppi version, and you can see just how important pixels are to print quality.

➤ **On-screen pictures:** For an on-screen photo, the number of pixels affects only the *size* at which the picture appears; the quality of the image is the same no matter what pixel count. (The Chapter 5 section related to Web images explains this issue fully.) A pixel count of 320 x 240 produces an image that displays at a size large enough for most on-screen purposes, including e-mail sharing.

75 ppi

200 ppi

So which pixel goal should you aim for when setting the camera's resolution? Unless you're sure that you will never print the photo, select a setting appropriate for printing. If needed, you can create a low-resolution copy of a high-resolution image in your photo editor (Chapter 5 shows you how). But you can't turn a low-resolution original into a good print by adding pixels, a process known as *resampling*. For example, to create the lion image to the right, I opened the 75-ppi image in my photo editor and added enough pixels to bring the image to 200 ppi. The result is no better and in some respects is worse than the low-resolution original.

The downside to high-resolution pictures is file size. The more pixels you capture, the more space the picture consumes on your camera memory card. As a point of comparison, the file size of the high-resolution lion (200 ppi) is 1.8MB (megabytes), but that of the low-resolution version (75 ppi) is just 140K (kilobytes). (A *byte* is a unit of computer data; 1K equals roughly 1,000 bytes, and 1MB equals about 1 million bytes.) Thankfully, memory cards are cheap now — you can get a 512MB memory card for under $40. So stock up and don't be stingy with the pixels.

To ensure that you'll be able to make good prints of your photos, take these steps:

❶ Multiply the print size by the desired resolution (ppi) to determine how many pixels you need.

The table to the right lists the approximate pixel counts required to print 200-ppi images at traditional frame sizes.

Julie's Take: I consider 200 ppi the *minimum* for most printers, but check your manual and run your own tests. Some printers require 300 ppi or higher, and some can get by with less than 200 ppi.

75 ppi resampled to 200 ppi

Resolution Requirements		
Print Size	*Pixels for 200 ppi*	*Megapixels*
4 x 6	800 x 1200	1 mp
5 x 7	1000 x 1400	1.5 mp
8 x 10	1600 x 2000	3 mp
11 x 14	2200 x 2800	6 mp

Capture More Pixels for Better Prints *(continued)*

2 **Increase the camera resolution if you plan to crop the image.**

You need more original pixels because you will trim some away in the cropping process.

When shooting the butterfly scene to the right, for example, I really wanted a tighter composition than what you see in the top image. But I couldn't capture a shot that included less background because I scared the butterfly away when I moved closer to it. Knowing that I would need to crop the image later, I set my camera to its highest resolution — 3008 x 2000 pixels. When I cropped the image to the composition you see in the second photo, the remaining image area measured 812 x 897 pixels, which gave me more than enough pixels to print a high-quality image at the size shown here.

3 **Set the resolution *before* you take the picture.**

Some cameras offer independent resolution control, as shown on the first menu here. Other cameras group resolution and file format (JPEG, TIFF, RAW) into a single control. These options are often assigned vague labels such as those shown on the second menu, in which case you must consult your manual to find out what format and resolution you get at each setting.

(See the upcoming section "Bury JPEG Artifacts" for more about file formats.)

Remember: Regardless of how your camera presents the resolution option, dial in this setting before pressing the shutter button. Again, you can't add pixels later to repair resolution-impaired photos.

3008 X 2000 pixels

812 X 897 pixels

Basic	Custom 1	Custom 2
Drive mode		
Image size	• 2048 x 1536	
Quality	1600 x 1200	
White balance	1280 x 960	
‹›Key func.	640 x 480	
	Menu ⟲	

SHQ	2272 x 1704	
HQ	2272 x 1704	
SQ1	2048 x 1536	
SQ2	640 x 480	▷
SELECT ⇨ ⬍		**GO ⇨ OK**

❹ Before printing, double-check the pixel count to make sure you select an appropriate print size.

Your photo-editing software may offer some guidance in this matter. In Photoshop Elements, for example, a warning appears in the Print Preview dialog box if you choose an inappropriate print size, as shown in the dialog box to the right. (This program sets 220 ppi as the print quality threshold; again, the best value depends on your printer.)

Most retail print kiosks and online printing sites offer similar alerts if your image file doesn't have enough pixels for the print size you chose. But if you're printing directly from a memory card on a home printer, you're responsible for selecting an appropriate print size.

You can check pixel count in any photo software. In Elements, open the image and choose Image➪Resize➪Image Size to open the Image Size dialog box. The pixel values — or *pixel dimensions* — appear at the top of the dialog box.

Note: In this dialog box, you also can select a specific print resolution and custom print size. If you do, be *sure* to deselect the Resample Image check box, as shown in the figure, to avoid adding or deleting pixels. See the Elements Help system for details.

To save yourself the trouble of opening the image, you can instead view the pixel count in a photo browser. In the Windows version of Elements, for example, open the Organizer and click on the image thumbnail to display the pixel count in the Properties panel, as shown here. (In Elements for the Mac, Adobe Bridge serves the same purpose as the Organizer.)

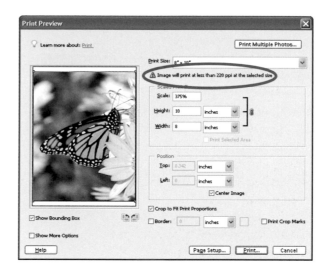

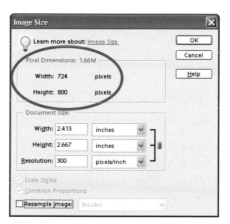

Chapter 1: Setting Up Your Camera and Digital Darkroom

Bury JPEG Artifacts

Depending on your camera, you may be able to choose the image *file format*. File format simply refers to the type of picture file that the camera creates. The three most common digital-camera file formats are JPEG (*jay-peg*), TIFF (*tiff,* as in spat), and Camera Raw (*raw,* as in uncooked).

On most cameras, JPEG is the default format — and for good reason. JPEG offers two distinct advantages:

➤ All Web and e-mail programs can display JPEG images, but TIFF and Camera Raw files must be converted to JPEG for online viewing.

➤ JPEG files also are much smaller than TIFF or Camera Raw files, allowing you to fit more pictures on your camera memory card.

The bad news is that JPEG achieves smaller file sizes through *lossy compression,* a process that throws away image data. With heavy compression, so much data is dumped that you wind up with the low quality you see in the top portrait here. Heavily compressed images have a tiled look and exhibit weird color halos — defects known collectively as JPEG *artifacts.*

Don't be totally put off by JPEG, however, or worry if your camera offers *only* JPEG. Most cameras offer two or more JPEG capture settings, each of which applies a different amount of compression. Lightly compressed photos look just fine, as evidenced by the bottom portrait.

Take these steps to keep compression problems at bay:

❶ Determine which JPEG settings on your camera produce an acceptable trade-off between compression and image quality.

The amount of compression applied at each JPEG setting varies from camera to camera. So take some test shots at each of the available settings on your model.

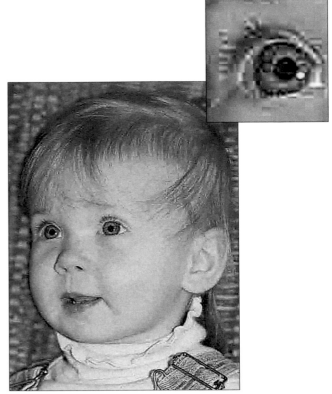

Heavy JPEG compression, 60K

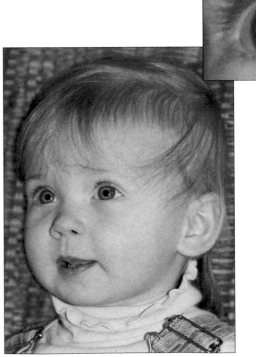

Minimum JPEG compression, 575K

On some cameras, you can select the file format independent of resolution, as illustrated in the left camera menu. Other cameras bundle format and resolution together, as indicated by the right menu. In both cases, the settings usually have vague names, such as Fine, Normal, and Basic. If your camera allows independent resolution control, test each compression/resolution combination.

Open the test images in your photo editor to evaluate how much damage occurs at each setting. Zoom in so that you can detect any artifacts.

Note: All the example images here were shot at the same resolution. If you combine heavy compression with low resolution, you exacerbate the damage.

❷ To avoid any compression, shoot in the TIFF or Camera Raw format instead of JPEG.

Remember that your files will be significantly larger. The file size of the TIFF portrait here, for example, is roughly five times larger than its high-quality JPEG twin. And, as illustrated by these examples, you may not see a huge quality improvement unless you print the picture very large. (The next section, "Go Raw for Maximum Quality and Control," explains Camera Raw; see Chapter 5 to find out how to convert TIFF and Camera Raw files to JPEG for online sharing.)

❸ If you edit your photo, save the altered file in the TIFF or PSD format, not JPEG.

If you resave your photo as a JPEG, it undergoes more compression. Instead, save edited photos in a format such as TIFF or PSD (the Photoshop format), which do not apply lossy compression. Save the picture in the JPEG format only if you need to use it online (or for some other on-screen purpose) and only after you finish editing it.

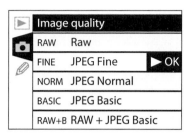

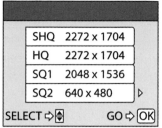

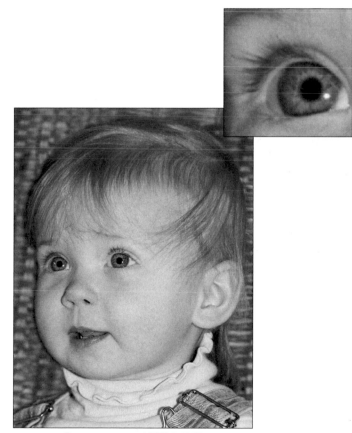

Uncompressed TIFF, 2.6MB

Go Raw for Maximum Quality and Control

When you shoot a picture in the JPEG or TIFF format, the camera applies some post-capture processing to enhance color, sharpness, and exposure. In most cases, the results of this automatic processing are good — great, even. But if your camera enables you to capture images in the Camera Raw format, you may want to experiment to see whether you can get better results by switching to that format.

With Camera Raw, you get pure, "uncooked" image data. After transferring the files to your computer, you use a piece of software known as a *Raw converter* to specify exactly how you want the raw data translated into a final image.

This option can be especially helpful in tricky lighting. For example, I took these pictures in a dental lab, in a room that was illuminated by fluorescent overheads and daylight shining through large windows. I also needed my camera's flash to get enough light on the dental mold. In the JPEG format, the camera's white balance mechanism got confused by the different light sources, causing image colors to be slightly off, as illustrated in the top image. (Chapter 4 explains white balance.) The JPEG image is also slightly oversaturated. With Camera Raw, I could set the white balance and saturation level myself to produce the more accurate colors you see in the bottom image.

In addition, because Camera Raw applies no file compression, you don't have to worry about the artifacts that can occur with the JPEG format. (See the preceding section for more on this topic.)

You do pay a price for Camera Raw, however. First, no compression means that Camera Raw files are significantly larger than JPEG files, which means that they eat up much more room on your camera memory card. Second, the Camera Raw conversion process takes time and effort. You can't edit your photo or share it online until you do the conversion and save a copy of the

JPEG, 500K

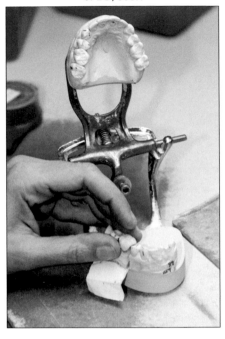

Camera Raw, 5MB

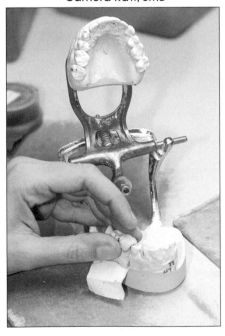

processed file in a standard photo format, such as TIFF or JPEG.

For times when you decide Raw is worthwhile, the following steps walk you through the conversion process. The steps feature the Adobe Camera Raw converter in Photoshop Elements 4.0; most Raw converters offer similar options.

❶ Choose File⇨Open and open the image file in the usual way.

Note: Camera Raw files have different Windows file extensions depending on the camera manufacturer. For example, Nikon Raw files have the extension .NEF, but the Canon extension is .CRW.

After you open the file, the Raw converter dialog box appears. The preview shows you how the image will look if you open it with the conversion settings selected in the panels on the right side of the dialog box. To zoom in on the image, click the Zoom tool icon and then click the image. Hold down the Alt key (Windows) or Option key (Mac) and click to zoom out. To scroll the image, drag in the preview with the Hand tool.

❷ Set the preview options.

Select the Preview, Shadows, and Highlights check boxes at the top of the converter window. When enabled, these options alert you that the conversion settings you've chosen will result in *clipped highlights* and *clipped shadows* — very light pixels will become white and very dark pixels will become black.

Clipped highlights are indicated in the preview with a red overlay; clipped shadows, with a blue overlay. In the example image, the preview shows some clipped highlights near the center of the photo, along the horizontal brass bar of the thingy that holds the dental mold. You can see some clipped shadows underneath the bar and along the thumb area.

Zoom and Hand tools   Preview options

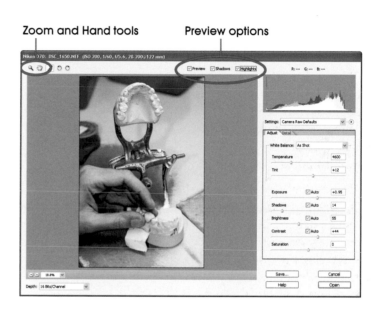

Go Raw for Maximum Quality and Control *(continued)*

❸ Select the bit depth from the Depth drop-down list in the lower-left corner of the dialog box.

A *bit* is a unit of computer data (8 bits equals 1 byte). *Bit depth* is a measure of how much color data an image file can hold. A standard digital camera image has a bit depth of 8 bits per channel — that is, 8 bits each for the red, green, and blue color channels in an image — or a total of 24 bits. (Refer to the appendix if this is your first encounter with the term *color channel*.)

Some cameras, however, can create images with 16 bits per channel, for 48 bits total. If your camera offers this option and you want to retain all 16 bits, select the 16 Bits/Channel option from the Depth drop-down list.

What's the benefit of higher bit depth? It's a long story, but the short answer is that 8-bit images sometimes exhibit a defect called *banding* or *posterization* if you subject them to extreme exposure or color adjustments in a photo editor. Color transitions that should be smooth and seamless become choppy. The blue background area in the 8-bit image here shows banding, for example. Banding is less likely to occur with 16-bit images.

Julie's Take: You may experience banding even in 16-bit images, however. In addition, most photo-editing programs either can't open 16-bit images or limit you to using just a few photo-editing tools. The additional bits also increase the image file size, which means that your photo editor will need more time (and power) to process your edits. So check your photo editor's Help system before you leap into 16-bit territory.

If you use Elements, I suggest that you open the image in 16-bit mode, make your exposure and color adjustments, and then convert the image to 8-bit mode before tackling any other retouching work. (Choose Image⇨Mode⇨8 Bits/Channel to do this conversion.)

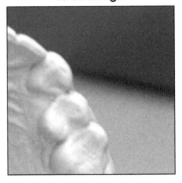

16-bit image

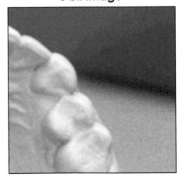

8-bit image

❹ Click the Adjust tab in the panel on the right side of the dialog box.

You should now see the controls shown in the figure to the right.

❺ Select Camera Raw Defaults from the Settings drop-down list.

The converter automatically applies the settings that the program thinks are best for your camera. You can see the changes that the automatic settings made to the dental lab photo here.

❻ Use the White Balance controls to remove any color cast.

Initially, the White Balance control is set to As Shot, which uses the white-balance setting the camera had in mind when you took the picture. (Chapter 4 explains white balancing in detail.) To adjust the white balance, you can choose a specific light source from the White Balance drop-down list or just drag the Temperature and Tint sliders until the color cast disappears.

With the Temperature slider, you can correct a blue or yellow color cast. Drag the Tint slider to remove a green or magenta color cast. The impact of moving either slider depends on the original light source. For the dental-lab shot, I used the settings shown here.

❼ (Optional) Adjust exposure with the Exposure, Shadows, Brightness, and Contrast sliders.

I typically don't take advantage of these options unless the preview indicates serious highlight or shadow clipping. You can

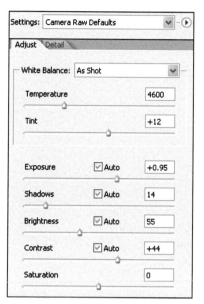

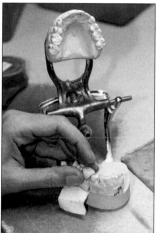

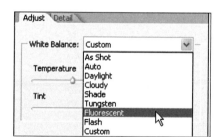

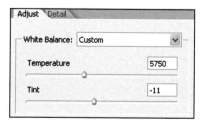

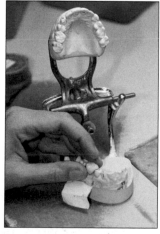

Go Raw for Maximum Quality and Control *(continued)*

manipulate exposure with much more precision after you open the photo in Elements proper. Not only do you get a broader selection of exposure tools, but you can apply changes to just the areas that need them, whereas Raw-converter adjustments affect the entire image. (See Chapter 2 for more on exposure adjustments.)

If you don't plan to edit your photo later or if you do see significant clipping, use the converter controls like so:

➤ **Adjust highlights:** Drag the Exposure slider to the right to brighten *highlights* (the lightest areas of the image); drag left to darken them.

➤ **Adjust shadows:** Drag the Shadows slider to the right to make the darkest areas darker; drag left to lighten them.

➤ **Adjust midtones:** In case you're new to the term, *midtones* are areas of medium brightness. Drag the Brightness slider to the right to brighten midtones; drag left to darken them.

➤ **Adjust midtone contrast:** Drag the Contrast slider to tweak contrast in the midtones.

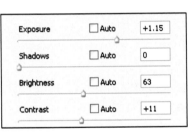

❽ Adjust color saturation if needed.

Drag the Saturation slider to the right to increase *saturation* (the intensity or purity of color). Drag left to decrease saturation. However, if you don't want to adjust all colors, wait to make this change until you open the image. You can then apply the Hue/Saturation filter to specific color ranges or to selected parts of the image. (Chapter 4 shows you how.) In the example image, the entire photo was oversaturated, so I lowered the Saturation value slightly.

❾ Click the Detail tab.

You get access to three more options. As with the settings on the Adjust tab, the converter initially sets the values for these options

according to what it thinks is appropriate for your camera. The dialog box here shows these settings for the camera I used.

⑩ Set the Sharpness value to 0.

Raising the Sharpness value creates the illusion of sharper focus by manipulating contrast.

Julie's Take: I suggest that you do not sharpen your image at this time, for two reasons:

> ➤ Sharpening should be done *after* you set the final image output size because the amount of sharpening needed varies depending on size.

> ➤ You get more control over the effect if you instead use the sharpening filter inside Elements. You can read more about sharpening in Chapter 3.

⑪ Use the Luminance Smoothing and Color Noise Reduction sliders to reduce image noise, if needed.

The Luminance Smoothing slider attempts to rid the image of so-called *luminance noise,* which gives a photo a grainy look. The Color Noise Reduction slider tackles *color noise,* which looks like bits of colored confetti. Noise is most often caused by very dim lighting, a too-high ISO setting, or a very long exposure.

Be careful when using either of the noise-removal options. They eliminate noise by blurring the image, and when over-applied, destroy image detail. My image didn't have a noise problem, so I set both sliders to 0 to avoid any blurring.

If you do apply the noise-removal options, zoom in closely on your image to monitor the effects as you drag the sliders.

Luminance Noise

Color Noise

Go Raw for Maximum Quality and Control *(continued)*

⑫ Click the Open button.

The converted image appears in the Elements workspace, as shown here.

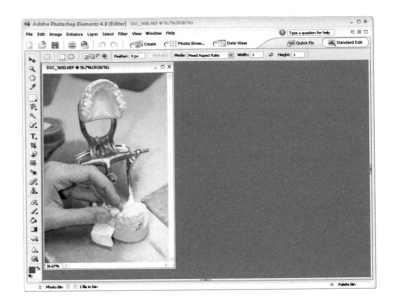

⑬ Choose File➪Save As to save your converted image.

If you don't save the image before closing it, you lose the converted version. Save the picture in the TIFF or PSD (Photoshop) format to retain all picture data. Do *not* save in the JPEG format; doing so applies lossy compression, which is destructive to the image.

Note that the Camera Raw dialog box also offers a Save button. If you click this button, you can save the converted file without opening it. However, Elements lets you save converted files only in the new Adobe DNG format. (See the Author Confidential for details.) Because not all programs can open DNG files, I recommend opening the file and saving it in the more widely recognized TIFF or PSD format instead.

Author Confidential

Is DNG the Next Big Thing?

Although the term *Camera Raw* is used in a generic sense, the truth is that no standard Camera Raw format yet exists. Instead, every manufacturer has developed its own proprietary format for raw images. This cornucopia of formats makes it difficult for software developers to support all types of Camera Raw files — a problem compounded by the fact that camera manufacturers often update their Raw formats as they introduce new models.

Industry experts worry that software makers may one day stop supporting Camera Raw files from less popular or older cameras, leaving photographers with hard drives full of useless files. To address this issue, Adobe recently introduced a new format, called DNG (for *Digital Negative*). The goal of DNG is to provide a raw-capture standard around which the imaging industry can unite.

Future cameras may offer DNG as an alternative to Camera Raw. In the meantime, you can take the preventative step of making DNG copies of your current Camera Raw files. Adobe offers a free DNG converter and more details about DNG at its Web site (www.adobe.com). The latest editions of Photoshop and Photoshop Elements also offer this feature.

Turn Off Digital Zoom

Most digital cameras offer *digital zoom*. This feature, although hyped in ads, in fact is destructive to image quality.

Digital zoom really should be called "in-camera cropping and enlargement," because that's what it does: The camera crops away the perimeter of the image and enlarges the remaining area to fill the frame.

Assuming that you shoot at a high resolution, this cropping might be okay because the cropped area would probably still contain enough pixels to produce a good picture. The problem is that the camera adds new pixels to the cropped image to give you the impression that your image was taken at the resolution setting you specified. And as you can see in the earlier discussion about resolution, adding pixels to an existing image usually makes it look worse. Zooming with a real zoom lens — an *optical zoom,* in technical terms — causes no loss of quality.

In addition, zooming with an optical zoom affects depth of field (the zone of sharp focus). When you zoom in, background objects appear blurrier; zoom out, and they appear sharper. This optical phenomenon, which enables you to manipulate focus according to your compositional goals, does not happen with digital zoom. Note the differences in focus between the background in the optical zoom example and the digital zoom example here; the background focus in the digital zoom example is unchanged from the original (top) image.

You can read more about working with an optical zoom in Chapter 3. For now, check your manual to see whether your camera offers a setting that permanently disables digital zoom. If not, the camera should alert you in some way when you transition from optical to digital zoom (assuming your camera offers both). When you see or hear that signal, back off on the zoom button to avoid damaging your pictures.

No zoom

Optical zoom

Digital zoom

Expand Your Palette with a Wider-Gamut Color Space

Some digital cameras offer a choice of *color spaces,* also known as *color models.* This setting controls the spectrum of colors, or *gamut,* that can be included in a photo.

The standard digital-camera color space is sRGB, which is based on the color palette that most computer monitors and printers can reproduce. In case you're wondering, the *s* stands for *standard,* and the *RGB* stands for *red-green-blue,* the three primary colors that are used to create digital images.

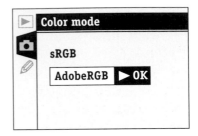

The idea behind sRGB is to improve color consistency as photos move from camera to monitor to printer. However, sRGB takes the lowest common denominator approach to achieve that goal, including only colors that are widely supported on all devices (which is why some people refer to sRGB as *small* RGB). In fact, some printable colors don't make the cut.

For photographers who object to the limits of sRGB, some cameras also offer one or more color spaces that encompass a broader color spectrum. The most popular of these so-called *wider-gamut* color spaces is Adobe RGB.

The illustration to the right offers an approximation of the colors encompassed by Adobe RGB and by sRGB. Neither space can render all the colors that the human eye can see; no imaging device has that capability. But Adobe RGB claims more of the visible spectrum than sRGB, especially in the green-cyan-blue arena.

How much difference you will actually notice if you switch to Adobe RGB depends on the colors in your picture, of course. In the images shown here, many colors look much the same in sRGB as they do in Adobe RGB. But some hues do vary — compare the pink mica powder at the bottom of the image, for example, and the red and green bricks of clay.

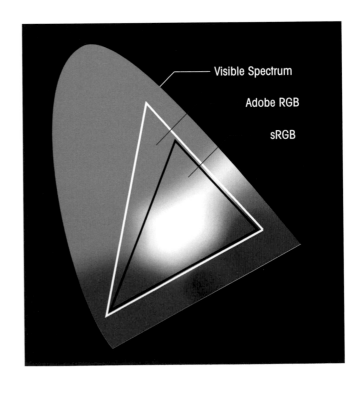

Keep in mind, too, that Adobe RGB does encompass some colors that may not ultimately be reproducible by your monitor or printer. Still, I see no reason not to capture the broadest color spectrum when you shoot — you've got nothing to lose, and color potential to gain.

Be sure that your photo software supports Adobe RGB, however. Some programs automatically convert images to sRGB when you open them, which sort of defeats the purpose of shooting them in larger color space. As you might expect, Photoshop Elements *does* support Adobe RGB. See the appendix of this book to find out how to take advantage of this feature in Elements.

Adobe RGB isn't the only alternative to sRGB, by the way. Depending on your camera, you may have the option of using other wide-gamut color spaces, including ProPhoto RGB or ColorMatch RGB.

sRGB

Adobe RGB

Frame Loosely for Greater Print Flexibility

This final camera-related tip ensures that after you capture a high-quality image, you don't wind up losing part of the picture when you print it at a traditional print size: 4 x 6 inches, 5 x 7 inches, 8 x 10 inches, and so on.

If you ever had your digital picture files turned into 4 x 6-inch prints, you may have noticed that your prints either don't include the entire original image area or include a margin of white around the perimeter of the print. Your photo printer isn't to blame; the problem is that 4 x 6-inch prints are based on film negatives, which have a 3:2 *aspect ratio* — that is, they're 3 units wide by 2 units tall (or vice versa, depending on the orientation of the picture). Most digital cameras, however, create images that have a 4:3 aspect ratio, which mirrors that of most computer screens.

When the aspect ratio of the print and image conflict, you must crop the image to fit the print dimensions. Alternatively, you can shrink the image and then leave a border of empty paper to fill the rest of the print. This problem isn't a digital-only issue, by the way; the same thing occurs when you try to turn a 3:2 film negative into a 5 x 7-inch or 8 x 10-inch print.

Either way, the solution is to frame your images with enough margin to allow for future cropping. As an example, the red boxes in the images here show how much of a 4:3 digital original could fit in a 4 x 6, 5 x 7, or 8 x 10-inch print. (Chapter 5 shows you how to crop to a specific print size.)

Some digital cameras do capture 3:2 images or offer the choice of shooting at the 4:3 or 3:2 aspect ratio. In that case, you can frame your pictures normally, assuming that you only want 4 x 6-inch prints. But again, if you move up to some larger frame size, the cropping issue remains.

4 X 6

5 X 7

The best advice is to simply get in the habit of framing your pictures a little more loosely than may look appropriate through the viewfinder. This strategy is especially important when you're shooting portraits — it ensures that you don't wind up chopping off someone's ears or eyebrows when you print the picture.

8 X 10

Author Confidential

Avoiding Parallax Errors

When you review your pictures on your camera monitor, you may discover that the area the camera captured is slightly different than what you saw through your viewfinder. This problem is most often caused by *parallax error,* a phenomenon that occurs with a viewfinder that shows you the scene from its own window rather than providing a *through-the-lens* preview. Because the viewfinder is above and to the left of the lens, its angle of view is not exactly the same as that of the lens. Most point-and-shoot cameras have this kind of viewfinder.

To avoid parallax errors, you can frame your image by using the camera monitor, which does offer a through-the-lens perspective. Or simply frame your picture loosely so that you ensure that you capture the entire subject.

Note that even with a through-the-lens viewfinder, the viewfinder and lens are never exactly in synch. Your camera manual should spell out how much the two diverge and how to frame your shots to account for the disparity.

Profile Your Monitor for Accurate Image Display

Tucked in a system file on your computer is a *monitor profile*. The profile is simply a data file that characterizes your monitor's color capabilities. When you open a digital photo, your computer uses the profile to decide how to most accurately render the image on-screen. The profile also plays a role in how color data is translated to your printer.

Unfortunately, the system profiles are generic to a type of monitor, not to your specific display. Because displays even of the same model can vary widely, generic profiles are often inaccurate. For a better solution, build a custom monitor profile. You can do this in several ways:

❶ If you use Photoshop Elements for Windows, run Adobe Gamma.

Adobe Gamma is a free monitor-profiling tool provided in the Windows version of Photoshop Elements.

To run Adobe Gamma, open the Windows Control Panel (click the Start button and then click Control Panel). Click the Appearance and Themes icon and then click the Adobe Gamma icon. When the window shown here appears, choose the Step By Step option, click Next, and follow the on-screen instructions.

❷ On a Mac, run the Display Calibrator Assistant.

Select System Preferences from the Apple menu to open the System Preferences dialog box. Click the Displays icon and then click the Color button. Choose your monitor from the Display Profile list and then click the Calibrate button. Again, a wizard appears on-screen to guide you through the rest of the process.

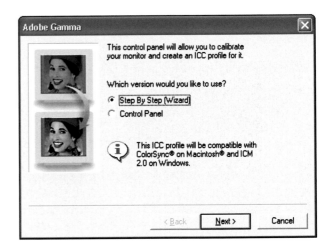

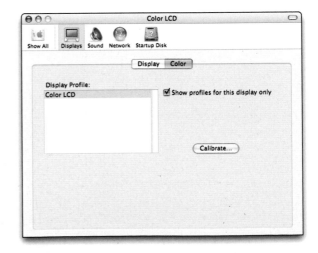

③ Invest in a commercial profiling package.

Both Adobe Gamma and the Apple Display Calibrator Assistant ask you to make visual judgments about color as you work through the profiling process. That isn't the most objective means of measuring the colors your display produces.

As an alternative, you can get a device known as a *colorimeter*. You stick the colorimeter to your screen, and it takes precise color measurements to build your monitor profile. The colorimeter shown here is from ColorVision; other well-known options are offered by X-Rite and GretagMacbeth. The devices, which start at about $90, ship with the software you need to build and install your monitor profile.

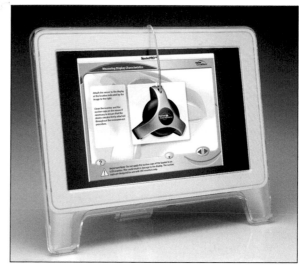

Photo courtesy ColorVision

Color by the Numbers

Creating a custom monitor profile is an important step toward better color accuracy. But if your photo software offers *color management* features, you may be able to go even further. Color management is too complex to cover fully in this book, but in a nutshell, it's a series of steps you take to better control how your computer handles color data as pictures move from camera to screen to printer.

To understand how color management works, you need to know that in an image file, colors are represented by numbers. But the exact color you get from any number depends on the device. On one monitor, the value that represents red might give you a bright, eye-popping red, for example, but another screen might deliver a less-saturated, darker red. In fact, every camera, scaner, printer, and monitor interprets color values slightly differently — and therein lies the heart of the color-consistency challenge that every digital photographer faces.

The first step in implementing a color-management system, or CMS, is to create profiles that characterize how each of your imaging devices interprets color values. When you add a printer or monitor to your system, the installation software adds profiles created by the manufacturer. You also can use *device independent* profiles — that is, profiles based on a generic color spectrum such as Adobe RGB or sRGB rather than a specific piece of equipment. But for greater accuracy, you can build custom profiles by using special software and calibration equipment. Either way, when you display or print an image, the CMS consults those profiles to figure out how to translate the color values to keep the colors as consistent as possible. (The appendix at the back of this book contains information on enabling the color management features in Photoshop Elements.)

Make Friends with Your Photo Editor

Some people say that using computer software to retouch digital photos is cheating. I say, baloney. Why toss away an image if all it needs is a little work in the digital darkroom? Besides, even the most famous photographers in history retouched some of their images. Today's photo software just makes the job easier (and less messy).

This book features one of the leading photo editing programs, Adobe Photoshop Elements 4.0, shown to the right here. (If you still use version 3.0, things look and work much the same.)

Although this book isn't intended to be a thorough guide to Elements, I want to share in the rest of this chapter a few basics that will help you complete the retouching projects featured in later chapters. To start with, here's how to select tools and adjust the picture display:

Toolbox

❶ To select a tool in the toolbox, just click the tool icon.

Don't see the toolbox? Choose Window⇨ Tools to display it. Depending on the size of the Elements program window, your toolbox may appear as a two-column palette instead of the single-column affair shown in the figure.

Note: In this book, I often show just a portion of the toolbox so that I can show the important elements at a larger size.

If you click the little black triangle in the bottom-right corner of some tool icons, you unfurl a flyout menu that contains additional tools, as shown to the right here. To use one of those tools, just click it. The flyout menu closes, and the selected tool's icon remains visible in the toolbox.

You also can switch between tools that share a toolbox slot by clicking the tool icons at the left end of the options bar, circled in the figure here.

Options bar

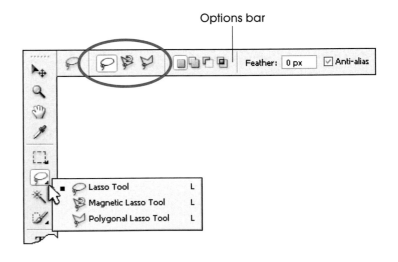

② Customize tool performance via the options bar controls.

See the next section for a primer on the most common tool options. You must set these options *before* using the tool — they have no effect after the fact.

③ Use the Zoom and Hand tools to adjust the image view if needed.

To magnify the display, click the image with the Zoom tool. To zoom out, hold down the Alt key (Windows) or Option key (Mac) as you click with the Zoom tool.

Drag inside the image window with the Hand tool to scroll the display so that you can see image areas that are currently not visible.

Customize Your Tool Brush to the Job

Some retouching tools are *brush based* — you swab them over your image as you might a paint brush. For these tools, you can adjust the tool tip, or brush, to suit the job at hand. I suggest specific brush settings in the projects later in the book; for now, acquaint yourself with these basics of customizing brushes.

Note: Some of the settings I mention here apply *only* to the Brush tool, which you use to apply paint. The Brush tool comes into play in several retouching projects, and I decided to explain its options up front so that I have more room in the later chapters to cover specific retouching techniques.

Follow these steps to customize your Brush tool:

① To set the initial brush size and shape, click an icon in the Brushes palette.

Open the palette by clicking the area circled in the figure to the right. To access the brushes that are most helpful for retouching work, choose Default Brushes from the Brushes drop-down list in the palette.

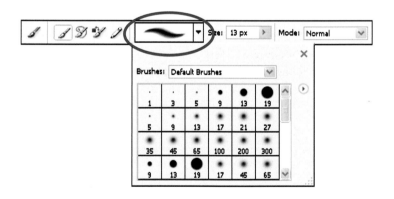

The numbers below each icon represent the brush diameter, in pixels. The fuzzy icons represent soft-edged brushes; the others represent hard-edged brushes. I explain more on that issue in Step 7.

(If your palette doesn't look like the one here, click the little triangle on the right side of the palette, and then choose Small Thumbnail from the pop-up menu.)

② Fine-tune the brush diameter by using the Size control.

Alternatively, you can use these keyboard shortcuts: To increase the brush diameter, press the right-bracket key (]). To reduce the brush size, press the left-bracket key ([).

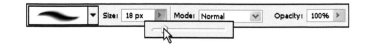

❸ Use the Mode control to adjust how edited pixels blend with the originals.

The Mode control affects the tool's *blending mode.* By changing the blending mode, you alter how your edited pixels — pixels that you touch with the editing tool — mix with the original image pixels.

For most retouching work, you use the Normal mode, in which the altered pixels completely obscure the original pixels. But other modes come in handy occasionally. In the first two butterfly illustrations to the right, for example, I painted part of the wing with the same color of blue in both images. In this case — actually, any time you want to change the color of an object by painting it — the Normal mode doesn't produce as realistic a result as the Color mode.

❹ Adjust the translucency of your brush strokes by changing the Opacity value.

At any Opacity value lower than 100%, your edited pixels become translucent, allowing your original pixels to remain partially visible. The lower the Opacity value, the more translucent your altered pixels become.

To see what I mean, take a look at the third butterfly image. Here, I painted again with blue, using the Normal mode, but lowered the Opacity value to 50%.

Customize Your Tool Brush to the Job *(continued)*

⑤ Disable the Airbrush option.

Some retouching projects in this book involve the Brush tool, which you use to paint color on a photo. The Brush tool offers an airbrush mode, which you toggle on and off via the Airbrush icon on the options bar.

When set to airbrush mode, the Brush tool behaves like a real airbrush: It pumps out paint as long as you hold down the mouse button. It's a nice feature for digital painting, but I recommend turning it off for photo retouching because you get more consistent, predictable, and controllable paint strokes in regular mode. (The icon should appear as you see to the right here.)

⑥ If you work with a pressure-sensitive tablet, explore the Tablet Options palette.

When the Brush tool is active, the options bar offers the Tablet Options palette, which you open by clicking the little triangle circled in the figure to the right.

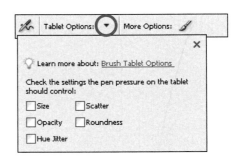

The palette controls relate only to users who work with a stylus and pressure-sensitive tablet instead of a mouse. Selecting a check box enables you to adjust that tool behavior simply by altering stylus pressure. I recommend *not* enabling these options until you're very familiar with the Brush tool. Otherwise, you may find it difficult to tell whether the tool is responding in a certain way because of pen pressure or some other tool setting. Note that the Size check box is selected by default, so visit the palette and deselect it the first time you pick up the Brush tool.

If you do a lot of photo retouching, a tablet is well worth the money, by the way. Precision editing becomes much easier (and gentler on the wrist). The leading tablet maker, Wacom, offers a sub-$100 model, the Graphire. Shown here, the Graphire is a good entry-level tablet option.

Photo courtesy Wacom Technology

❼ Refine brush hardness in the More Options palette.

Brush *hardness* refers to whether your brush creates a hard-edged stroke or a soft-edged stroke. The lower the Hardness value, the fuzzier the stroke becomes, with paint fading out toward the edges.

In the Brushes palette (refer to Step 1), the fuzzy icons represent soft brushes, and the hard-edged icons represent hard brushes. In the palette, however, you get only brushes that are fully hard or fully soft — no in-between. But if you click the brush icon on the More Options palette, you get access to the Hardness slider, which enables you to choose any hardness setting from 0 (maximum softness) to 100 (maximum hardness).

Don't mess with the other controls in the palette unless you know what you're doing. They're geared mostly toward digital painting, not everyday photo retouching.

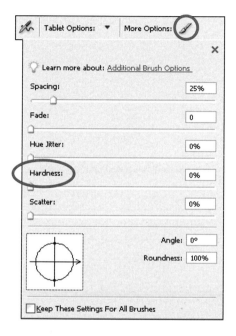

Author Confidential

Match Your Cursor to Your Brush Size

By default, the Photoshop Elements cursors look like the tool icons. You see a little paintbrush cursor when working with the Brush tool, for example. These cursors stay the same size no matter what brush diameter you use, so you have no way of knowing exactly how much area you'll affect with each swipe of your brush. The icon cursors can also obstruct your view when you're doing close-up work.

For a better way to work, choose Edit⇨ Preferences⇨Display and Cursors in Windows. On a Mac, choose Photoshop Elements⇨Preferences⇨ Display and Cursors. Set the Painting Cursors option to Full Size Brush. Now when you use any painting tool, your cursor is an empty circle that reflects the diameter of your brush. Also set the Other Cursors option to Precise to see a crosshair cursor instead of the tool-icon cursor when you work with tools that aren't brush-based. (Note that a few tools, such as the Zoom and Hand tools, always retain the icon cursor, however.)

Choose Your Paint Colors

When you work with Elements tools or effects filters that apply color to an image, you specify the colors you want to use via several controls found in the toolbox.

You can have two colors active at a time: the *foreground paint color* and the *background paint color.* You can set the paint colors in several ways:

❶ Click a toolbox color swatch to open the Color Picker.

At the bottom of the toolbox, you see four color controls, shown to the right here. The two large swatches indicate the current foreground and background colors.

Click the top color swatch to set the foreground color; click the bottom box to set the background color. Either way, you next see the Color Picker dialog box.

Inside the dialog box, make sure that the Only Web Colors check box is *not* selected. Click the H button to set up the dialog box as you see it here. Then drag or click in the vertical slider to select a basic hue; drag or click in the large color grid to adjust brightness and saturation.

The two large swatches at the top of the dialog box show you the color you're about to select (top) and the current foreground or background color (bottom). A third, tiny color box may appear to the right of the large swatches, as in this figure. The tiny box alerts you that your color is outside the so-called Web-safe spectrum. Read the upcoming sidebar to find out more about this issue (and why you can ignore it).

Click OK to close the Color Picker when you're happy with your color.

❷ Click a color in your image with the Eyedropper.

This method is the best way to match your paint color to a color in your image. To set

Foreground Color

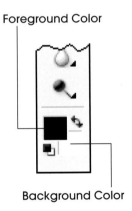

Background Color

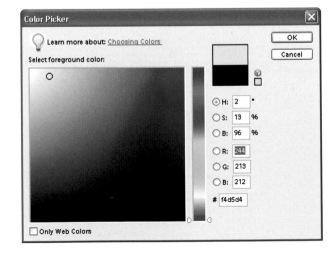

the foreground color, click in the image window with the Eyedropper, circled in the figure to the right. To set the background color, hold down the Alt key (Windows) or Option key (Mac) as you click.

If you set the Sample Size control on the options bar to Point Sample, the Eyedropper sets the color to match the exact pixel you click. You can also select a color that's an average of several neighboring pixels by using the 3 by 3 Average or 5 by 5 Average setting.

❸ To swap the foreground and background colors, press X.

Alternatively, if you have trouble remembering keyboard shortcuts, you can click the curvy double-headed arrow located just to the right of the foreground color swatch.

❹ To return to the default paint colors (black and white), press D.

Clicking the little mini-set of color swatches, circled in the figure to the right, accomplishes the same thing.

What's a "Web-Safe" Color?

Most computers today ship from the factory set to display more than 16 million different colors. But if you dig into your system controls, you can limit the display to 256 basic colors. If the system then encounters a color outside that spectrum, it substitutes the closest available color. This color-swapping can make even simple graphics appear blotchy, and it's downright disastrous for photos. So why would anyone do it? Because lowering the number of colors the computer has to display speeds the system performance.

Some Web designers stay within the 256-color palette when creating page backgrounds, text, and the like so that their sites look as good as possible even at the lowest display setting. Thus, the 256-color spectrum is said to be *Web safe*. When you select paint colors as you retouch photos, however, don't worry about this issue. Your photo probably already contains *lots* of colors that aren't Web safe, and one more isn't going to make a difference. Also, very few people still run their monitors at the 256-color setting, so the chances that anyone will view your picture with that limited palette are slim.

Master the Art of Selecting

On many occasions, you may want to apply a corrective filter or other change to just a portion of your photo. For example, I wanted to slightly adjust the glass in the church window to restore the warm glow that originally drew my eye to this scene. You begin this type of selective editing by using a *selection tool* to enclose the area you want to change in an outline, officially called a *selection outline*.

Julie's Take: Photoshop Elements, like most photo programs, offers a variety of selection tools. Some of them, however, are not very precise, are difficult to use, or come in handy only once in a blue moon. So this section and the next one cover the two selection tools that are the most useful on a daily basis: the Selection Brush and the Magic Wand. You can get the basics of using one other selection tool, the Rectangular Marquee tool, in the cropping discussion in Chapter 5.

With that explanation out of the way, allow me to introduce you to the Selection Brush. With this tool, you can precisely select even the most complex subject. You use it like so:

❶ Click the Selection Brush icon in the toolbox.

The Selection Brush shares a slot in the toolbox with the Magic Selection Brush, so be sure to grab the right tool.

❷ On the options bar, set the Mode control to Mask.

In Mask mode, the tool works like a paintbrush. You paint over the areas that you *don't* want to alter. In the imaging biz, this is known as *masking*. The concept is the same as when you apply that liquid masking stuff on your window panes before painting the trim — you're laying down a protective coating that prevents the area from being altered.

③ Make sure that the Subtract from Selection icon on the options bar is selected.

It should be selected by default, but double-check just to be sure. Don't be confused by the icon name: When you choose Mask mode, Elements automatically selects the entire image, even though you don't see a selection outline. So when you apply the mask paint — which is what you're about to do — you subtract the areas you paint over from that selection. If you click the icon to the left, named Add to Selection, Elements covers the entire image with a mask as soon as you click the image, and then you paint to remove the mask.

Note: This setup and these two icons are new to version 4.0; in version 3.0, the tool simply applies the mask paint any time you're in Mask mode.

④ Select a brush from the Brushes palette.

If you need help with this step, see the earlier section "Customize Your Tool Brush to the Job." For this task, just choose any of the round brushes found in the first row of the palette. You can fine-tune the brush size and hardness later.

⑤ Set the Hardness value.

Just like the Hardness value for the Brush tool, this value controls whether the Selection Brush paints soft-edged or crisp strokes. (Again, refer to the prior section about customizing your brush tools for details.) If you use a soft brush, the edit you apply after finishing the mask fades out at the edges of the selected area. With a hard brush, the alteration has a clear-cut edge.

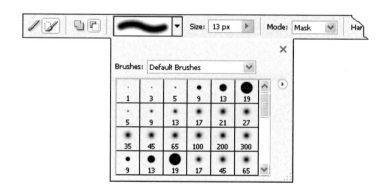

Master the Art of Selecting *(continued)*

To show you an example, I selected a portion of the church image and pasted it into a new background. For the left image, I created the mask with a hard brush. For the second, I used a soft brush. Notice that the boundary between the background and image is crisp in the example created with the hard brush and slightly blurred in the other.

Whether you should work with a soft or hard brush depends on the edit you're planning to make. Sometimes, a soft selection outline helps an alteration blend better with the original image. Other times, a hard-edged outline works better. This decision will become more clear to you as you gain experience with selecting.

For fully hard strokes, set the Hardness value to 100%. For the softest strokes, set the value to 0%.

❻ Paint along the edge of the area you want to mask.

Drag to paint a stroke; click to lay down one brush-full of paint. Zoom in close so that you can get a good view of the area you're painting as shown on the right.

Note: By default, the mask appears as a red, translucent overlay. You can adjust the mask display by using the Overlay Opacity and Overlay Color controls at the right end of the options bar.

You may need to adjust the brush size as you paint to get the mask into any nooks and crannies along the edges. You also may need to adjust brush hardness periodically because some segments of the outline may call for a softer or harder brush. For example, I painted with a hard brush along the boundary between the window and the wood. But when painting over the cross, I reduced the Hardness value to 0% because

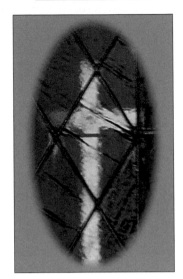

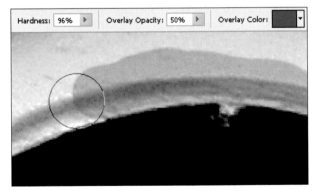

the cross is softly focused — there is no clear boundary between the cross and the glass, and I didn't want to create one by applying an exposure correction that had a distinct edge. The illustration to the right shows you the mask boundary I painted, presented here without the underlying image to make the mask edges easier to see.

❼ If you mess up, set the tool to paint-remover mode.

You do this by clicking the Add to Selection icon on the options bar, circled in the figure to the right. Then just drag over the areas you want to unmask — which adds those areas to the selection you ultimately will produce.

Alternate Method: For an even quicker option, leave the Subtract from Selection icon selected and simply hold down the Alt key (Windows) or Option key (Mac) as you drag over the pixels you want to unmask. When you release the key, the tool returns to applying mask paint.

❽ Paint over the rest of the area to be masked.

Continue until the entire area you don't want to alter is masked, as shown in the illustration to the right. To speed things up, switch to a larger brush so that you can cover more ground with fewer strokes. For this portion of the mask, change the Hardness value to 100%. If you work with a soft brush at this stage, you risk leaving some pixels unmasked.

❾ Change the Mode control to Selection.

Master the Art of Selecting *(continued)*

Don't panic — the mask is supposed to disappear. In its place, you see a blinking, dashed outline, called a *selection outline*. Anything *inside* the outline is *selected* and thus will receive the impact of your next edit. Any pixels formerly under the mask are not selected and so will not be altered. You can see my final selection outline in the image to the right.

❿ (Optional) Save the selection outline.

If you spent a long time creating your mask, save the selection outline so that if you ever need it again, you don't have to redo the whole process. Elements stores the outline as part of the image file.

To save an outline, choose Select⇨Save Selection. Inside the Save Selection dialog box, select New from the Selection drop-down list, enter a name for the outline, and click OK.

When you need the outline again, choose Select⇨Load Selection. You then see the Load Selection dialog box. Select the outline from the Selection drop-down list, click the New Selection button, and click OK.

Note: To take advantage of this feature, you must save the file in the Elements native format, PSD, or in the TIFF format. Otherwise, the saved selection outline is dumped when you close the image.

Wave the Magic Wand to Select by Color

If the area you want to alter sports a consistent color throughout, you can save time by using the Magic Wand to select it. For example, you might use the Magic Wand to select the blue areas in an image. You simply click a blue pixel, and the Magic Wand selects similarly colored pixels. Here's the step-by-step process:

❶ Click the Magic Wand icon in the toolbox.

You also can activate the tool by pressing W.

❷ Click the New Selection icon on the options bar.

Circled in the figure to the right, this icon tells the tool that you want to start a new outline.

❸ Use the Tolerance and Contiguous controls, both on the options bar, to set the tool limits.

These controls work in tandem to determine the area selected by the wand.

➤ **Tolerance** controls how sensitive the tool is to color differences. With a low value, only pixels very similar to the one you click become selected.

➤ **Contiguous**, when enabled, tells the Magic Wand to select pixels only if they are *contiguous* to the one you click — that is, if no differently colored pixels lie between them and the clicked pixel. When Contiguous is off, the tool selects all pixels that fall within the Tolerance range, regardless of their position in the image.

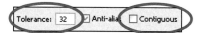

Wave the Magic Wand to Select by Color *(continued)*

To get a better feel for how the controls work, take a look at the examples to the right. I created four selection outlines, each time clicking at the area marked by the red bull's-eye in the top image but using different Tolerance/Contiguous combinations.

For the first selection outline, I set the Tolerance to 35 and turned the Contiguous option on. The bright yellow areas show you the extent of the resulting outline. (In real life, the outline appears as a blinking, dashed line; I filled the selection with color to make the illustration easier to understand.)

With these settings, the Magic Wand found very few qualifying pixels to select. Raising the value to 125 grabbed more pixels, as shown in the second illustration. But the selection is still limited to the single blue pot of mica powder because it is surrounded by white pixels. Other pixels in the image meet the Tolerance value, but they're not selected because they're non-contiguous to the original pixel I clicked.

For the lower pair of images, I again used 35 and 125 as the Tolerance values but disabled the Contiguous option. Now qualifying blue pixels throughout the image are subject to selection.

As you might expect, the tool selected the greatest area when I used the higher Tolerance value and turned off the Contiguous option.

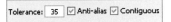

④ (Optional) Select the Anti-Alias check box.

Anti-aliasing smoothes the jagged edges that can occur along diagonal or curved segments of a selection outline. The examples to the right give you a close-up look at the anti-aliasing effect.

For most projects, anti-aliasing is a good thing. But it does blur the edges of the outline slightly, so if you want an extremely precise outline, turn off this option.

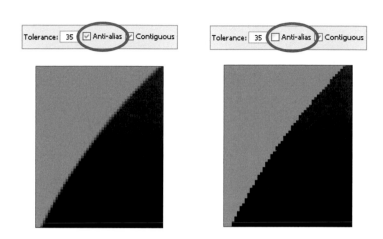

⑤ Select the Sample All Layers check box to base the selection on all layers.

Did that sentence make you say "Huh?" If so, ignore this option; it applies only to multilayer images. Unless you added layers after opening your photo, it contains only one layer. If you're layer savvy, on the other hand, you can tell the Magic Wand to consider pixels on all layers by turning on the Sample All Layers option.

⑥ In the image window, click the color you want to select.

A blinking selection outline appears. Any pixels inside the outline are selected.

⑦ Adjust the outline if needed.

If the tool didn't select the area you had in mind, adjust the tool options and try again. When you click, the original selection outline goes away and a new one appears.

Alternatively, you can add to the existing outline: Click the Add to Selection icon and then click another color. Or forget the icon and just press Shift as you click.

To subtract from the selection, click the Subtract from Selection icon and then click the color you want to deselect. Or bypass the icon and Alt+click (Windows) or Option+click (Mac) instead.

2

EXPOSURE AND LIGHTING MAKEOVERS

All cameras, from top-of-the-line digital wonders to simple pinhole models, are based on the same basic idea: An image is captured when light is focused through a lens onto a light-sensitive recording medium.

Over the years, that recording medium has evolved from specially-coated copper plates to silver-halide film to the chip-based image sensors used in today's digital cameras. But whatever the technology, the photographer's primary challenge is exposing the recording medium to just the right amount of light. Too much light, and the photo will be too bright. Not enough light, and the picture will be too dark.

You have a huge advantage over early photographers, of course. Thanks to the autoexposure features provided on modern cameras, you can simply press the shutter button and let the camera do the exposure calculation.

More often than not, that calculation is dead on. But for the times when the camera makes a decision that's off the mark, you can use the techniques in this chapter to solve the problem. Additionally, you'll find out how to get better results when the situation calls for a flash or other artificial light source.

For times when you don't get a good exposure despite your best efforts — trust me, it happens to *every* photographer now and then — this chapter also shows you how to use photo-editing tools to improve your image.

Exposing a Better Picture

You can approach exposure problems from several directions. To figure out the best solution, you need a basic understanding of the main factors that determine exposure: *shutter speed, aperture,* and *ISO.*

In case you're new to these terms, here's a quick primer:

➤ **Shutter speed:** The *shutter* is a light barrier in front of the image sensor. When you press the shutter button, the shutter opens briefly to allow light to strike the sensor. *Shutter speed* controls how long the shutter remains open. Shutter speed is usually stated in fractions of a second, as in 1/320 second.

➤ **Aperture (f-stop):** The *aperture* is a hole in an adjustable diaphragm between the lens and the shutter. The aperture setting, stated in *f-stops,* controls the size of that hole and thus how much light passes through the lens as shown in the illustration to the right.

➤ **ISO:** Introduced in Chapter 1, the ISO control adjusts the camera's sensitivity to light. The higher the ISO, the less light you need to produce a good exposure.

To sum up, shutter speed and aperture control how much light hits the image sensor, and ISO determines how strongly the sensor reacts to that light. So:

➤ For a brighter image, you decrease the shutter speed, open the aperture, or increase ISO.

➤ For a darker image, you increase shutter speed, reduce the aperture size, or lower ISO.

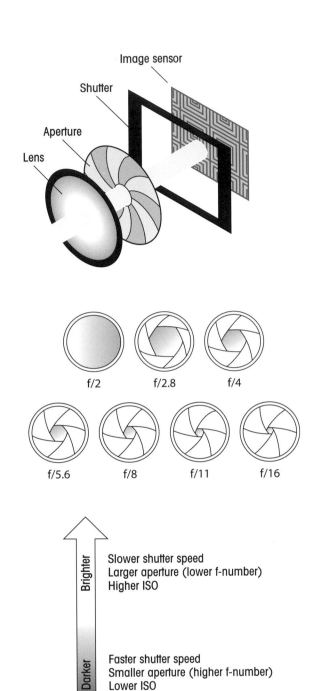

Image sensor

Shutter

Aperture

Lens

f/2   f/2.8   f/4

f/5.6   f/8   f/11   f/16

Brighter

Slower shutter speed
Larger aperture (lower f-number)
Higher ISO

Darker

Faster shutter speed
Smaller aperture (higher f-number)
Lower ISO

Most cameras offer a few different ISO settings, but the extent to which you can control aperture size and shutter speed varies. Check your manual to find out which of the four exposure-control modes listed in the table to the right are available to you.

Even if your camera offers only programmed autoexposure (AE), you may have some input into shutter speed and aperture. Many cameras offer *scene modes* or *creative modes,* which are automatic modes that produce certain f-stops or shutter speeds. Some cameras even offer scene modes plus all four exposure control modes. Scene modes are usually represented by icons like the ones shown on the control dial to the right: a head or torso for Portrait, a moving figure for Action, and so on.

The burning question now is this: Is there one "best" combination of aperture, shutter speed, and ISO? As far as image *brightness* goes, the answer is no. You can achieve the exact same brightness through any number of combinations of the three settings.

However, aperture, shutter speed, and ISO each affect *other* aspects of your photo differently:

➤ Aperture affects *depth of field* (the zone of sharp focus).

➤ Shutter speed determines whether moving objects appear sharply focused.

➤ ISO is related to an image defect known as *noise,* which Chapter 1 explains.

Whether you should approach your exposure issue from the point of aperture, shutter speed, or ISO depends on which of these side effects best suits your picture:

Exposure Control Modes		
Mode	*Symbol*	*How It Works*
Programmed Autoexposure	P or Auto	Camera sets aperture and shutter speed
Aperture-Priority Autoexposure	A or Av	User sets aperture; camera sets shutter speed
Shutter-Priority Autoexposure	S or Tv	User sets shutter speed; camera sets aperture
Manual	M	User sets both shutter speed and aperture

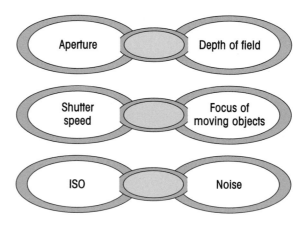

Scene modes

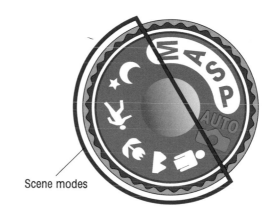

Exposing a Better Picture *(continued)*

❶ To shift depth of field with exposure, adjust the aperture.

Depth of field refers to the zone of sharp focus in an image. As you open up the aperture — by selecting a *lower* f-stop number — objects at a distance appear less focused.

As an example, I shot the underexposed Before image, featuring the man of my house, at an ISO of 200, a shutter speed of 1/320 second, and an aperture of f/7.1. For the first After photo, I opened the aperture to f/4. Notice that the change not only corrected the exposure problem but also caused the grass in the background to be in softer focus.

Alternate Method: If you want the shortened depth of field that a larger aperture produces but your camera doesn't offer manual control or aperture-priority AE, try Portrait scene mode. This mode automatically uses the largest aperture possible because most portraits look best with a softly focused background. For a smaller aperture, try Landscape mode, which is designed to produce the sharpest background possible.

You also can manipulate depth of field by changing the lens focal length or the camera-to-subject distance. Chapter 3 explains these options.

❷ To affect the focus of moving objects as you shift exposure, adjust the shutter speed.

With a slow shutter, moving objects may appear blurry in the picture. As an example, I exposed the third dog image at 1/60 second. My baby was posing pretty patiently,

ISO 200, f/7.1, 1/320

Before

ISO 200, f/4, 1/320

After

but his panting and the wind in his fur were enough to blur the image at this shutter speed. To eliminate the blur, I raised the shutter speed to 1/125 second, opening the aperture to compensate for the faster shutter.

Alternate Method: To force a faster shutter on a camera that doesn't offer manual control or shutter-priority autoexposure, try using Action scene mode. Note that if you move your camera during the exposure, still objects may also appear blurry, especially at slow shutter speeds.

Chapter 3 contains additional information about this issue and using shutter speed to affect focus.

❸ Raise ISO as a last resort.

The tradeoff for the increased light-sensitivity of high ISO is the possible introduction of image noise, a defect you can see in Chapter 1. For this reason, shoot at the lowest ISO when possible and rely on aperture and shutter-speed adjustments for exposure control.

ISO 200, f/18, 1/60

ISO 200, f/11, 1/125

After

Autoexposure Hack #1: Change the Metering Mode

Autoexposure works remarkably well in most situations. But in certain lighting conditions, autoexposure may not deliver the picture you had in mind.

If your camera offers manual exposure, you can adjust aperture, shutter speed, or ISO to solve the problem. But changing these settings in program autoexposure (AE), aperture-priority AE, or shutter-priority AE doesn't work. When you change one setting, the camera adjusts the others to produce the same exposure — the exposure that *it* thinks is appropriate.

You aren't without power to manipulate exposure, however. First, check your manual to find out whether you can adjust the auto-exposure *metering mode*. This control lets you specify what area of the frame the camera should consider when calculating exposure. The three standard modes — pattern, center-weighted, and spot — are usually represented by the icons in the table.

The default mode, pattern — sometimes called *matrix*, *multi-zone*, or *average metering* — works fine for most images. But when the background is significantly darker or lighter than the foreground, as in the Before images, this mode can result in an under- or overexposed subject. In this scenario, try one of the other two modes:

Metering Mode	Symbol	Exposure Based On . . .
Pattern		Entire frame
Center-weighted		Entire frame, more emphasis on center
Spot		Center of frame

Pattern metering

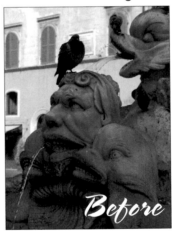

Author Confidential

Metering Modes for Manual Exposure?

Even in manual-exposure mode, most cameras assist you by displaying an exposure guide in the viewfinder or on the monitor. The guide reflects the metering mode, so set the mode to reflect the exposure you have in mind.

❶ Choose center-weighted metering to give more emphasis to the middle of the frame.

Center-weighted metering factors the entire frame into the exposure equation, but gives more importance to the center of the frame.

In the fountain photo, this mode resulted in some lightening of the image, but it didn't completely correct the exposure of the fountain. But in the flower image, center-weighted mode offered a good balance between flower and background.

❷ To base exposure solely on the center of the frame, use spot metering.

Spot metering produced the best exposure for the fountain photo. But in the flower image, the petals remain too hot because the center of the frame is mostly dark. (The size of the area evaluated in spot-metering mode varies; check your manual for specifics.)

Note: You can use spot metering even if your subject isn't at the center of the frame. Frame the scene with the subject in the center, press and hold the shutter button halfway, reframe, and then press the shutter button the rest of the way.

Center-weighted metering

Spot metering

Autoexposure Hack #2: EV Compensation

If your camera doesn't offer metering-mode control or if changing the metering mode doesn't resolve the exposure problem, try applying *exposure-value compensation,* better known as EV compensation. EV compensation simply tells the camera that you want a darker or lighter picture than what its autoexposure system thought was appropriate.

Almost every digital camera offers this feature. To use it, follow these steps:

❶ Locate the EV control.

The EV control is usually labeled with a little +/− symbol like the one highlighted in the middle skyline image. Settings typically range from −3.0 to +3.0, with a value of 0.0 resulting in no exposure adjustment. You typically can step the exposure up or down in half or third steps: +0.3, +0.7, +1.0, and so on. However, the amount of exposure change that occurs at each increment depends on your camera.

❷ For a darker exposure, lower the EV setting.

For my sunset image, an EV setting of 0.0 kept the buildings properly exposed. But I wanted a darker exposure to emphasize the drama of the darkening skyline illuminated by the bright city lights. In addition, the vertical light tower near the center of the frame was much too bright in the first exposure. An EV setting of −2.0 produced the exposure I liked best.

In case you're wondering: No, there is no way to darken the foreground and keep the background the same, or vice versa. But you can make this adjustment in most photo editors. Just follow the Chapter 1 instructions for selecting the area you want to alter before you apply your exposure correction.

EV 0.0

EV −1.3

EV −2.0

❸ For a brighter exposure, raise the EV setting.

My skeleton picture also needed a little help in the exposure department, this time in the opposite direction. All the white and bright yellows in the image caused the autoexposure meter to produce a slightly dark image. Raising the EV setting to +0.7 corrected the problem.

Note: How your camera arrives at the exposure you request through EV compensation depends on which autoexposure mode you use:

➤ **Aperture-priority mode:** The camera adjusts shutter speed (so that it can stick with the aperture setting you requested). In dim lighting, the shutter speed may be slow, so use a tripod to avoid blurring that can result from hand-held camera shake during a long exposure.

➤ **Shutter-priority mode:** The camera shifts aperture in response to the EV setting. Remember that aperture also affects depth of field.

➤ **Program autoexposure:** The camera may adjust either aperture or shutter speed; you're out of the decision-making loop.

For all three modes, the camera may also adjust ISO if you set the ISO control to Automatic mode — which I strongly advise *against* for reasons you can explore in Chapter 1.

Keep in mind, too, that EV compensation can go only as far as the camera's shutter speed and aperture limits allow. Even the highest EV setting, for example, can't produce a good exposure without adequate lighting.

EV 0.0

EV +0.3

EV +0.7

Go Flash Free for Better Indoor Portraits

Unless you're a professional photographer or dedicated amateur, your "lighting equipment" probably consists of the pop-up flash built into your camera. Although certainly convenient, a built-in flash is ill-suited to the purpose for which most people use it: taking indoor pictures of family and friends.

The problem with a built-in flash is that the light it produces is harsh and narrowly focused. For portraits (as well as for close-ups of objects), this leads to a couple of problems. First, the light is too strong and unevenly distributed, producing *hot spots* — overexposed areas — like you see on the forehead and apples of the cheeks in the Before photo.

A built-in flash typically also produces severe shadows behind your subject. In the Before image, this shadowing isn't a major problem because my friend is sitting very close to the sofa cushion — there's little space for a shadow to emerge. Still, the strong line of shadow behind the ear takes emphasis away from the eyes, which should be the focal point for any portrait. And speaking of eyes, a built-in flash nearly always produces red eye, as it did here.

Although you usually can't avoid using a flash at night, you can achieve better daytime portraits by using this technique:

❶ Position your subject next to a window.

For my portrait image, I pulled open the window blinds and drapes to allow the maximum light into the room.

❷ Pose the subject so that one side of the face is illuminated by the window light.

Most people have a hard time not squinting if they are looking directly into the light. So having the light shine on the side of the face usually works best.

Built-in flash

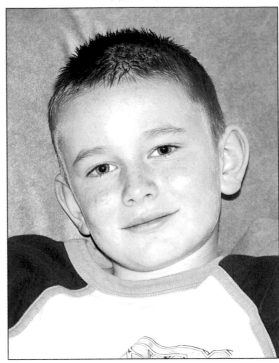

❸ Open the aperture as much as possible.

The larger the aperture, the faster the shutter speed you can use. If the aperture is *stopped down* — that is, you select a high f-stop to reduce the size of the aperture — you may need such a slow shutter speed to get a good exposure that the slightest movement of the camera or subject will blur the image.

For portraits, opening the aperture (choosing a lower f-stop number) has the beneficial side effect of shortening depth of field, which means that your portrait background will be in softer focus. (See Chapter 3 for more on this issue.)

To specify the aperture, you must switch the camera to manual-exposure mode or aperture-priority mode, usually indicated by the letters *A* or *Av*. If your camera offers only automatic exposure, set the camera to Portrait mode, if available. That mode, usually indicated by a head or torso symbol, also chooses a wider aperture. However, some cameras don't allow you to disable flash in Portrait mode, so it may not be an option for this technique.

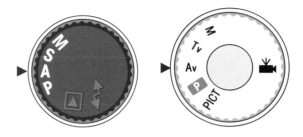

❹ Turn off the on-board flash.

In automatic mode, the flash will fire unless the room light is very, very strong. So check your manual to find out how to turn off the flash. The universal symbol for "no flash" is a lightning bolt with a slash through it, as shown to the right.

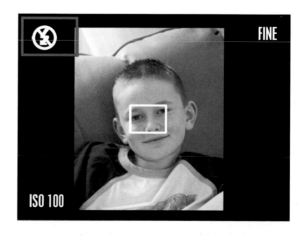

Go Flash Free for Better Indoor Portraits *(continued)*

⑤ Snap a test shot.

If the room and window light together are very bright, you may be satisfied with your results. But often, the unlighted side of the face will remain too shadowed and the overall exposure not quite right. You can see my initial flash-free attempt to the right. The window side of the face is a little too bright, and the rest of the face is underexposed.

⑥ Use a reflector to bounce window light onto the shadowed side of the face.

A reflector is nothing more than a white, gold, or silver panel that you use to reflect light. For this type of portrait, you position the reflector so that it catches the window light and bounces it back onto the shadowed side of your subject, as shown to the right.

Reflectors are inexpensive and are available in most camera stores. They come in a variety of sizes and colors; the product shot to the right shows an assortment from Photoflex (www.photoflex.com). The color of the reflector influences image colors somewhat; a gold reflector slightly warms skin tones, for example, and a silver reflector cools colors a bit. My reflector is actually gold on one side (the side facing my subject in this image) and white on the other.

Alternate Method: If you don't want to invest in a reflector, a piece of white poster board can do the trick. You can even create a reflector by covering a piece of cardboard with silver or gold foil.

No flash

Courtesy Photoflex, Inc.

❼ Reshoot, evaluate, and adjust exposure and/or add more light if needed.

If your shot remains a little dark even with a reflector, try these solutions:

➤ Turn on additional room lights, moving them as close to your subject as possible. Check the image colors after your next shot, however. When a scene is lit both by daylight and artificial light, the camera's white-balance mechanism can get confused. If colors look off, switch to manual white balance and experiment to find the setting that provides the most neutral colors. Chapter 4 discusses white balance in detail.

➤ In manual-exposure mode, select a slower shutter speed. In aperture-priority mode, select a higher EV compensation setting. Assuming that you already have the aperture open to its maximum, the camera reduces shutter speed to increase the exposure. You can also raise EV in autoexposure mode or Portrait scene mode: The camera may adjust shutter speed or aperture to provide the brighter exposure.

Be careful about slowing the shutter speed too much. With a longer exposure time, any movement óf the subject or camera will produce blurring. See Chapter 3 for more tips on shutter speed.

➤ If absolutely necessary, raise the ISO setting. Remember, though, that a higher ISO typically adds image noise, a defect illustrated in Chapter 1.

For my portrait, the reflector alone added just the right pop of light to produce a great exposure. And because I used a gold reflector, the skin tones received a nice bit of warmth, as well.

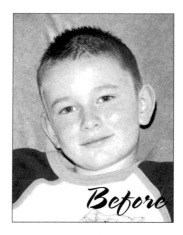

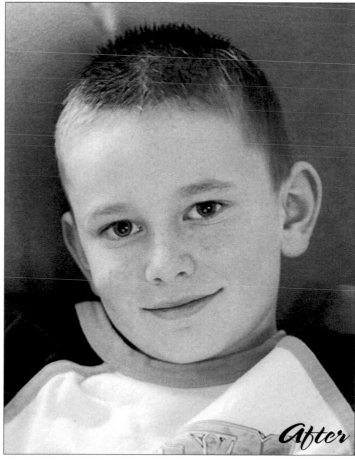

No flash, reflected window light

Use Fill Flash to Improve Outdoor Portraits

For the reasons I explain in the preceding makeover, I try to go without flash when taking indoor portraits. But for outdoor portraits, I rarely shoot *without* flash. And that goes for both nighttime and daytime photos.

Adding flash at night makes sense, but why the need to supplement daylight? Well, any time your light comes from above the subject — as it does when you're shooting by sunlight — the ridge of the brow can cast shadows that obscure the eyes. The problem is exacerbated if your subject happens to be wearing a hat or hood, as in my Before picture.

Your first instinct might be to use one of the techniques I cover earlier in this chapter to produce a brighter exposure. But that would produce an overall exposure shift, which isn't what you need here. Even if you used EV compensation, for example, to brighten the image, the eyes would still be in shadow relative to the rest of the face — and the brightest parts of the scene might become overexposed.

With a flash, you can add a small pop of light just to the face. And, here's the good news: That little built-in flash that does such a lousy job indoors works just fine for this purpose, where it serves as a secondary light source.

To use flash outdoors successfully, you need to know just a few tricks:

❶ Position your subject within range of the flash.

Your camera manual should tell you how far the flash light will reach. If your subject is

Before

beyond that range, flash won't do you any good. For example, there's no point in using flash to snap a picture of your baseball-playing teen rounding third if you're sitting hundreds of feet away in the stands.

❷ Set the flash to fill flash mode.

By default, the flash is set to automatic mode, which means that the camera reads the light and determines when the flash is needed. In bright light, the flash won't fire in automatic mode, so you need to select whatever mode forces the flash to fire no matter what the lighting conditions.

Depending on your camera, this mode may be called *fill flash* or *force flash*. Usually, you see a little lightning bolt icon like the one in the figure to the right. (Make sure that the word *Auto* doesn't appear next to the flash icon.)

❸ If colors appear too warm or too cool, adjust the white balance setting as necessary.

When you enable the flash, your camera automatically chooses the white balance setting appropriate for the color of flash light. Depending on the overall lighting conditions, the result may be warmer (more golden) or cooler (more blue) skin tones. For my portraits, the result was a slight warming effect, which worked well for this subject.

If you don't like the color shift, switch to manual white balance and select a setting that produces more neutral tones. Chapter 4 explains white balance in detail.

Snap a More Colorful Sunset Portrait

No photo album of a beach vacation is complete without at least one shot of you or a traveling companion framed by a beautiful sunset (or sunrise, if you're that up-at-dawn-for-a-jog type). Unfortunately, most sunset portraits turn out looking like these two Before shots. Either the sky is stunning but the subject is underexposed, or the subject is properly exposed and the sky is so bright that it no longer displays any of the colors that you wanted to remember.

Here's the secret to capturing a sunset or sunrise portrait where both subject and sky are properly exposed:

❶ Set your camera to fill flash mode.

Also known as force flash, this mode ensures that the flash will fire even if the camera doesn't think it's necessary.

Alternate Method: Your camera also may offer a fill flash with red-eye-reduction mode. In this mode, the camera fires a little preflash before the actual flash. The preflash causes the subject's pupils to constrict, which lessens the chances of red eye. You can experiment with this flash setting at night, but be sure to warn your subject not to move until the actual flash goes off. Otherwise, the subject might blink or move just at the time the picture is being recorded.

If the sun hasn't set too far, you shouldn't need to worry about red eye because the pupils will have already constricted in response to the daylight.

Courtesy Annabelle Wallnau

Courtesy Annabelle Wallnau

❷ Watch out for lens flare.

Any time your lens is pointed toward the sun, you're at risk for lens flare, a defect shown to the right. The best way to prevent it is to use a lens hood, which works like an awning around the lens. Many cameras ship with a hood. You can also just cup your hand over the top of lens, moving it around until the flare disappears.

❸ Turn the ISO setting down as low as possible.

As detailed in Chapter 1, a higher ISO allows you to shoot in less light but also increases the chance of noise, the defect that gives your image a speckled look. If ever noise is going to be visible, it's in a shot like this, where there are no details in the background to obscure it.

❹ Take the picture at several different exposure settings.

Don't rely on your monitor for a completely accurate rendition of image brightness. To be on the safe side, *bracket* your shots: After you get one picture that looks good on the monitor, take a couple at a darker exposure and a couple at a brighter exposure.

If you're working in automatic-exposure mode, use the EV compensation control to produce darker or lighter images.

After

Courtesy Annabelle Wallnau

Banish Reflections and Shadows from Product Shots

You need a picture of an antique camera that you want to sell in an online auction. Or maybe you're participating in an art fair, and the publicity person wants to publish a photo of the jewelry you make in the fair's marketing flyer. You don't need anything fancy — just a straightforward shot that shows your product clearly.

Sounds easy enough, right? But when you try to capture the image, you discover that lighting your simple product shot isn't so simple after all. Your flash produces uneven lighting and a distracting shadow behind the camera. Stage the camera next to a lamp or window that offers enough light to go without flash, and you still get that darned shadow. On the jewelry shot, any light source at all produces reflective glare that not only creates a flare but also changes the colors in the beads.

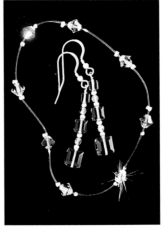

Professional photographers avoid these problems by using some special lighting equipment. If you do a lot of product or still-life shooting, you may want to invest in a few of these tools for your home studio, but you also can cobble together homemade solutions. The following tips explore both options and help you show any object in its best light (har har):

❶ Turn off the on-board flash.

Sorry, but your camera's tiny built-in flash is never going to produce good results; the light it emits is too harsh and too narrowly focused. So find whatever flash control you need to push or select to turn off the flash. Remember that the universal symbol for *no flash* is the lightning bolt with the slash through it, as shown to the right.

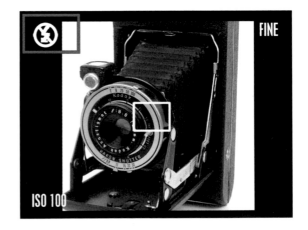

❷ Light your shot with lamps that produce soft, even light.

For photographers who are new to lighting (and who don't have a huge equipment budget), the best options are as follows:

➤ Professional-grade lamps such as the Lowel Tota-Light, shown to the right (www.lowel.com), use high-wattage bulbs — 300 to 750 watts for this model — and feature *barn doors,* which are flaps that you can adjust to control the spread of the light. A second popular studio-style lamp resembles a clip-on shop light but uses a high-wattage photo bulb. The model shown here is from Smith-Victor (www.smithvictor.com).

Expect to spend at least $100 for a light housing and the bulb; you'll also need to buy a good stand on which to mount the lamp.

Note: High-watt bulbs produce great light, but as you might expect, they get *hot.* So use caution when handling them and never light heat-sensitive products (or people) for long periods.

➤ An external flash head may also be a solution, assuming that your camera has a connection for attaching one. Make sure that the flash you buy allows you to angle the head so that the light strikes the wall or ceiling behind the subject and bounces down to cast the softest, broadest light.

If your camera doesn't accept an accessory flash, you can buy a *slave* flash unit, which is a flash head that fires when it senses the light from your on-board flash. This option can work well in some cases, but because you're forced to fire that problematic on-board flash, it isn't optimum.

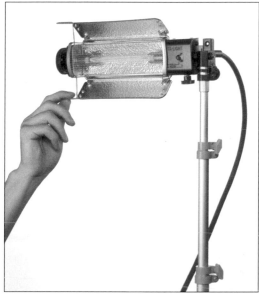

Courtesy Lowel-Light Manufacturing, Inc.

Courtesy Smith-Victor Corporation

Banish Reflections and Shadows from Product Shots *(continued)*

➤ Not ready to invest in professional lighting or a flash yet? Well, if you happen to have one of those clip-on shop or desk lamps, give that a try. For the best results, visit your camera store and buy a photoflood bulb, making sure that you don't exceed the wattage limit of the lamp.

Note: All these lighting solutions may cause a slight color cast if you leave your camera's white balance set to Auto. To remedy the problem, switch to manual white balance and cycle through the available settings to see which one neutralizes the colors. See Chapter 4 for more on white balance and how to remove a color cast.

❸ Diffuse the light with a tent, a dome, or an umbrella.

Good lights are just half of the product-photography equation. Even with a professional-grade studio lamp, you must find a way to diffuse the light to avoid reflections and soften shadows. Once again, you can buy professional diffusing products or make your own:

Courtesy Cloud Dome, Inc.

➤ For small objects, consider a product such as the Cloud Dome (www.cloud dome.com), shown in the top image to the right. You put your object inside the dome, position your lights around the outside, and shoot through an opening in the top. You can mount your camera to the bracket atop the dome, eliminating the need to use a tripod. Flexible light cubes offer a variation on the theme; the one shown here is also from Cloud Dome.

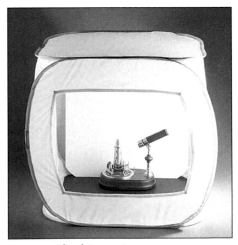

Courtesy Cloud Dome, Inc.

➤ For larger products, you can buy a light tent, which looks sort of like a teepee made out of white fabric. Again, you shoot through an opening in the tent, with your lights outside. You can buy tents in various sizes; the one shown to the right is from Lastolite (www.lastolite.com).

➤ If you buy studio lights, add diffuser umbrellas to the rig. These are simply translucent umbrellas that you attach in front of the light, as shown to the right. The umbrellas are inexpensive — about $30 — and you also can buy a light kit that includes light, stand, and umbrella. The kit shown to the right is from Lowel.

➤ In a pinch, you can use a gauzy white curtain or sheet to act as your light diffuser. Pieces of frosted glass can also work. However, trust me when I say that if you do a lot of product photography, you'll save yourself some time and hassle by investing in a real diffuser product.

Courtesy Lastolite Limited

Courtesy Lowel-Light Manufacturing, Inc.

Author Confidential

Photography Equipment Resources

I'm lucky to live in a town that has a professional photography store with a national reputation (Roberts Imaging, www.robertsimaging.com). If you don't have access to such a store, I can recommend several online sellers in addition to Roberts Imaging: B&H Photo Video (www.bhphotovideo.com), Samy's Camera (www.samys.com), and Calumet Photographic (www.calumetphoto.com).

Banish Reflections and Shadows from Product Shots *(continued)*

4 **Instead of aiming a single light directly at your subject, use two lights, one on either side.**

This cross-light setup gives you the best chance of both eliminating shadows and avoiding reflections. Working with two lights also allows you to put more distance between the object and the bulbs, further diffusing the light.

To produce the After camera shot, I used two lamps, both fitted with umbrellas. You can see my little makeshift studio to the right. For the jewelry shot, I put the bracelet and earrings inside a Cloud Dome and used my lamps without the umbrellas.

Before

After

Before

After

Correct Exposure in Your Photo Editor

No matter how sophisticated your camera or how adept your photography skills, you're bound to wind up with an under- or overexposed image every now and then. Not to worry: You can tweak exposure with very little effort in your photo-editing program.

Note, however, that I said "tweak." If your picture is so underexposed that nearly all pixels are black or so overexposed that half are white, don't expect to convert that clunker into a properly exposed image.

Most photo editors offer a basic filter that offers a single slider for adjusting brightness. (The Elements version is called Brightness/Contrast.) Although easy to use, the filter adjusts all pixels by the same amount, which may not be what you need. In the zebra image, for example, the highlights (brightest regions) and midtones (areas of medium brightness) are fine; only the shadows are too light. And in the portrait, the shadows are okay, but the midtones and highlights could use a brightness bump.

For a better solution, look for a *Levels* filter. With Levels, you can darken shadows, brighten highlights, and adjust midtones independently. (If you instead need to brighten shadows or tone down highlights, see the next makeover.)

The following steps show you how to use the Levels filter. To adjust only part of your image, follow the instructions in Chapter 1 to select that area before you start.

Correct Exposure in Your Photo Editor *(continued)*

① Choose Enhance⇨Adjust Lighting⇨Levels.

The Levels dialog box appears. Select RGB from the Channel drop-down list. Also select the Preview check box so that you can see the results of your exposure correction in the image window.

② Evaluate the histogram.

A *histogram* is a graph that plots image pixels on a brightness scale that ranges from 0 (black) to 255 (white), with shadows on the left and highlights on the right. A peak in the histogram indicates lots of pixels at that brightness value; a valley or flat line indicates few or no pixels.

For example, the histogram in the dialog box is for the zebra image. It shows no pixels at the left end of the histogram, reflecting the fact that the image is weak in the shadow department.

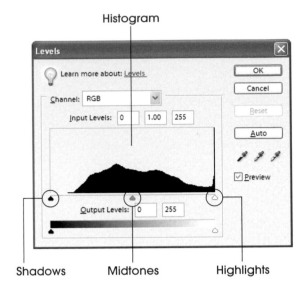

Histogram

Shadows   Midtones   Highlights

Author Confidential

Don't Let the Histogram Rule

Some photographers insist that the only acceptable exposure is one that results in an even distribution of pixels across the whole histogram, which indicates a perfect balance of shadows, highlights, and midtones. That's an entirely acceptable photographic goal, but it's not the only way to go. For example, a low-contrast picture, which produces a histogram with most pixels clustered in the middle, might be a better artistic choice for some subjects. So consider the histogram a valuable exposure guide, but not the final word on how you should expose an image. Also, if you use a newer, higher-end camera, you may be able to display a histogram on the camera monitor as you review an image.

❸ To darken shadows, drag the Shadows slider to the right.

Drag the leftmost slider to the point where the histogram indicates some pixels. Any pixels that originally fell at the brightness position of the slider become black, and other pixels are redistributed along the rest of the brightness spectrum.

For the zebra image, I dragged the Shadows slider from its original position (top figure) to the start of the histogram mountain (lower figure). You see the result in the images below.

When you move the Shadows or Highlights sliders, the Midtones slider moves in tandem. You can then reposition the Midtones slider if necessary. For my final zebra image, I left the slider alone, allowing midtones to darken slightly.

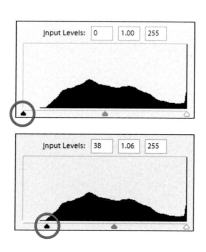

Correct Exposure in Your Photo Editor *(continued)*

④ To brighten highlights, drag the Highlights slider to the left.

Again, drag the slider to the spot where the histogram indicates the presence of some pixels. Pixels previously at the brightness position of the slider become white, and other pixels are remapped along the rest of the brightness scale.

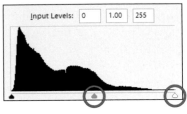

⑤ To adjust midtones, drag the middle slider.

Drag the slider left to brighten midtones; drag right to darken them.

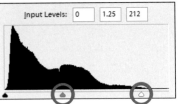

The figures to the right show the before and after positions of the midtones and highlights sliders for the portrait image. The final results appear below.

⑥ Click OK.

Applying the Levels filter sometimes has the unwanted side effect of desaturating colors. If you notice a meaningful color loss, follow up with an application of the Hue/Saturation filter, covered in Chapter 4.

Reveal Lost Shadow Detail

When you shoot *high-contrast* images — pictures that feature both very bright and very dark areas — exposing both the shadows and highlights properly is sometimes impossible.

In pictures taken at sunrise or sunset, for example, the foreground is typically dark, but the sky is light, as in this Before image. Boosting the exposure enough to adequately expose the foreground blows out the details in the sky. So if you want that sky, you're forced to forget about the foreground.

That foreground isn't necessarily lost forever, though; you may be able to rescue it in your photo editor. In Elements, the tool for making this correction is the Shadows/Highlights filter. Use it like so:

① Choose Enhance⇨Adjust Lighting⇨Shadows/Highlights.

The Shadows/Highlights dialog box appears, with the Lighten Shadows control set to 25%. You see an immediate brightening of the image.

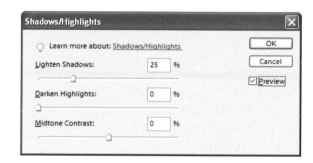

Author Confidential

Expose for the Highlights

When shooting sunsets, sunrises, and other scenes that contain both very bright and very dark regions, it's usually best to *expose for the highlights* — select exposure settings appropriate for the brightest areas — and then try to lighten any underexposed areas in your photo editor. Correcting overblown highlights in a photo editor is difficult, but you often can rescue shadow detail that may appear lost to the naked eye.

Reveal Lost Shadow Detail *(continued)*

② Drag the Lighten Shadows slider to the right as needed.

You can also tone down highlights by using the Darken Highlights slider. To adjust contrast of the midtones, use the Midtone Contrast slider.

For this image, I set the Lighten Shadows control to 34. I was happy with the existing highlights and midtone contrast, so I left those values unchanged.

③ Click OK.

You can see the dramatic impact of this filter in my After bridge image. Just this small shift brought out the formerly obscured blues of the water and added some extra pop to the trees.

Note: Many images may require a pass through both the Shadows/Highlights and Levels filters. Chapter 6 offers an example of how to use the two filters together.

How Bright is Bright Enough?

When you adjust the brightness of your photos in your photo-editing software, keep the picture's intended use in mind. Pictures usually appear darker in print than they do on-screen, so an image that looks fine on your computer monitor may need tweaking to look right in print. On-screen photos typically also appear darker on a Windows-based computer than on a Macintosh system, for reasons I won't bore you with. So if you are prepping images for a Web page, you need to find a brightness level that straddles the middle of the Windows/Mac fence.

Don't make *any* changes to image brightness — or to photo colors, for that matter — until you calibrate your monitor, however. Otherwise, you aren't evaluating the image on a neutral canvas, which means that you may adjust the image incorrectly. Chapter 1 explains the vital step of monitor calibration.

3 FOCUS MAKEOVERS

You may be surprised to find an entire chapter devoted to the subject of focus. What's the big deal, after all? Today's high-tech autofocusing systems pretty much do all the heavy lifting, right?

Well, in most cases, autofocus *does* work remarkably well (and this chapter shows you how to cope should you encounter a subject that stumps your camera). But good photographers do more than simply ensure that the main subject is in focus; they also use focus as a compositional element. As the makeovers in this part illustrate, you can use focus to direct the viewer's eye to a certain area, minimize a distracting background, emphasize motion, and add drama to an otherwise ho-hum shot.

Although a camera that offers manual focusing gives you the most creative flexibility over this aspect of your pictures, even an autofocus model provides more opportunity for input than you may think. This chapter offers autofocus tricks you can use to adjust how much of a scene is in sharp focus, for example. For times when you need a little after-capture focus touchup, this chapter also shows you how to sharpen or blur portions of your image in your photo editor.

Draw Attention to Your Subject with Focus

In a perfect world, you'd be able to set up all your photographs so that your subjects are beautifully staged against complimentary backgrounds. But unless you're shooting a studio portrait or still life, having that kind of control is rare.

Consider my shot of the lion statue, for example. This beast perches at the edge of a tall monument that overlooks the city of Indianapolis. There's absolutely no other angle from which to shoot him, short of hanging off the side of the building like Spider-Man. So if you want that lion, you get those buildings, which draw the eye away from the subject.

I faced a similar dilemma when shooting the butterfly image, where the tall background plant diverts attention to the top center of the scene. Had I reached in to remove the foliage, I surely would have scared the little guy (girl?) away.

Although you can't do away entirely with a busy background in situations like these, you can at least diminish its impact on your subject. The trick is to use camera settings that result in a short *depth of field*.

Depth of field refers to how much of a scene is in sharp focus. With short depth of field, the object on which you focus the lens is sharply focused, but objects at a distance are blurry. As the distance from the subject increases, so does the blur. And the blurrier an object becomes, the less it distracts the eye from the main subject.

Long Depth of Field   Short Depth of Field

You can manipulate depth of field in three ways:

➤ Adjust the aperture.

➤ Change the lens focal length.

➤ Change the distance between camera and subject.

If your goal is to shorten depth of field, leaving only your subject in sharp focus, use the following techniques:

❶ Select a lower f-stop to open the aperture.

Explained fully in Chapter 2, the aperture controls how much light strikes the image sensor while the shutter is open.

But the aperture setting — f-stop — affects depth of field as well as exposure. The larger the aperture, the shorter the depth of field.

Compare the two lion images to the right, for example. I took the first shot, which is the Before image, at f/20. For the second image, I opened the aperture to f/5.6. (Remember: A *lower* f-stop number produces a *larger* aperture.) The background buildings are noticeably less sharp in the f/5.6 version.

Julie's Take: One way to remember the relationship between focus and aperture is to envision the *f* in *f*-stop as also referring to *focus range.* The higher the number, the greater the range of sharp focus. (In case you're curious, the *f* really is related to the fact that the f-stop is a ratio between the size of the aperture and the lens focal length, which I explain in the next step.)

42mm, f/20, 1/60 second

42mm, f/5.6, 1/800 second

Draw Attention to Your Subject with Focus *(continued)*

Keep in mind that you must use a faster shutter speed to compensate for the additional light allowed in by the larger aperture. (In aperture-priority mode, the camera adjusts shutter speed automatically for you.)

To specify the aperture setting, switch to manual-exposure control or aperture-priority control. Manual exposure is usually indicated on control dials by the letter *M;* aperture priority, by *A* or *Av* (for *aperture value*).

Alternate Method: If your camera doesn't offer manual-exposure or aperture-priority control, look for a Portrait mode, usually labeled with a symbol that looks like a person's head or torso. This mode automatically uses a large aperture because blurry backgrounds are preferred in portraits.

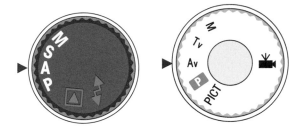

② If your camera has a zoom lens, zoom in as far as possible.

As you zoom, you increase the lens *focal length.* Measured in millimeters, focal length determines how much area your lens can capture and how large subjects appear in the frame. A camera with a 3X optical zoom typically offers focal lengths in the 35 to 100mm range. (Your camera manual should specify the exact range of your lens.) Keep these facts in mind:

➤ As focal length decreases, the camera captures a wider area, and objects appear smaller and farther away.

➤ As focal length increases, objects appear closer and larger, and less landscape is visible in the lens.

Compare the original lion photo (the Before photo on the next page), taken at a focal length of 42mm, with the version at the right, shot at 95mm. As you can see, zooming in has two benefits as far as diminishing a distracting background. First, you

95mm, f/20, 1/60 second

include less of the background in the scene. Second, a longer focal length also creates the illusion of a shorter depth of field.

Keep in mind that zooming also changes the spatial relationship between foreground and background objects, which may or may not be to your liking. For example, the tip of the lion's nose appears level with the top of the far-left background tower in the wide-angle (42mm) images, but in the zoomed (95mm) image, it appears at about the middle of the tower.

Note: These lens phenomena occur *only* with a true optical zoom lens, not with digital zoom. (For more about digital zoom, see Chapter 1.) Also, focal lengths in this book are stated as 35mm film-camera lens equivalents; see the upcoming Author Confidential for an explanation.

Of course, if you zoom in to capture a closer view of the subject *and* open the aperture, you get an even greater impact on your background. I used this tactic to shoot my After lion image, using a focal length of 95mm and an aperture of f/5.6. (The final depth-of-field reducer, moving closer to the subject, wasn't possible for this image.)

❸ Get closer to your subject.

Depth of field becomes greater as you put distance between the lens and the subject (assuming that you don't zoom in to compensate for moving farther away). So to minimize depth of field and make the background as blurry as possible, just move closer.

42mm, f/20, 1/60 second

95mm, f/5.6, 1/800 second

Draw Attention to Your Subject with Focus *(continued)*

Again, this option wasn't open for the lion image; I was already as close as I could get and still fit the entire structure in the frame. For the butterfly image, on the other hand, getting closer was my *only* option.

When I shot the Before image, the aperture was already wide open, and at a focal length of 300mm, I was maxed out as far as zooming. So I crept as quietly as I could closer to the butterfly, and amazingly, it remained posed long enough for me to capture the After shot. Both the Before and After shots appear to the right at the same size so that you can better compare their differences.

In the After image, some of that big plant in the background is still visible, but from this perspective, it's less focused and less intrusive. Of course, just like zooming in, repositioning does change your composition, which may not serve as well for all your subjects as it did for this one.

Blur a Busy Background in Your Photo Editor

If you can't shorten depth of field as you'd like by adjusting your camera settings (as described in the previous makeover), you can fake the effect in a photo-editing program. For example, I actually prefer the composition of the wide-angle lion images from the preceding makeover to the zoomed versions, but I wanted the background to be as blurry as it was in the final, zoomed After image. No problem, because I can simply apply a blur filter in my photo software to just the background.

The following steps show you how to create this effect in Photoshop Elements. You can use the same approach no matter what software you use, although the exact tool and filter names may vary.

❶ Select the background.

If you want to apply a change to just one portion of your image, you must first select that area. Elements offers a variety of selection tools, but in most cases, I prefer the Selection Brush. See Chapter 1 for details on using this tool.

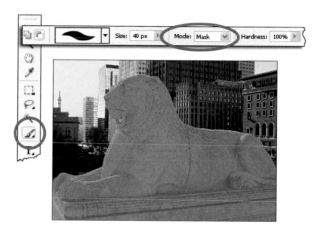

After grabbing the Selection Brush from the toolbox, set the Mode control on the options bar to Mask. Then paint a red mask over the lion, as shown in the middle figure to the right. A hard brush works best for this subject.

When the mask is complete, set the Mode control on the options bar to Selection. Now the mask disappears, and a dotted selection outline appears around everything that wasn't covered by the mask, as shown in the bottom figure to the right. In other words, your background is now selected.

Blur a Busy Background in Your Photo Editor *(continued)*

② Copy the selected background to a new layer.

To do this, choose Layer⟹New⟹Layer via Copy. If you display the Layers palette (Window⟹Layers), you can see the background copy in the layer thumbnail, as shown to the right here. (In Elements, the checkerboard pattern indicates empty areas of a layer.)

③ Choose Filter⟹Blur⟹ Gaussian Blur.

You see the Gaussian Blur dialog box. Select the Preview check box so that you can view the blur effect in the image window.

④ Adjust the Radius slider until you achieve the blur you want.

I set the value to 3.0 for the lion image. Don't worry if the blur effect seems eat into the edges of the subject a little; you can fix the problem later.

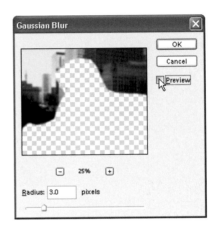

⑤ Click OK.

The dialog box closes.

⑥ Inspect the border between the subject and the background.

Zoom in for a close look. If you're happy with the picture, move on to Step 9. Otherwise, tackle Step 7.

⑦ Use the Eraser tool to wipe away any blurred subject pixels.

If the blur affected any of your subject pixels, pick up the Eraser tool. Choose a small, hard brush and set the Opacity control on the options bar to 100%. Make sure that the blur layer (the top layer) is still highlighted in the Layers palette, as shown to the right; if not, click the layer name. Then just drag over the blurred subject pixels. As you erase, the original, unblurred pixels from the layer below become visible.

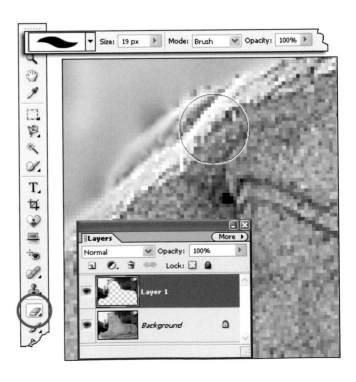

⑧ Use the Blur tool to blur any background areas you missed.

The Blur tool enables you to blur pixels just by dragging over them, as if you were rubbing Vaseline on a lens. Select the tool from the toolbox, set the Mode to Normal, set the Strength value to 30%, and turn on the Sample All Layers check box. Working again on the top (blur) layer, drag over areas you want to blur. If one pass of the tool doesn't produce enough blur, simply wipe over the pixels again.

⑨ Choose Layer⇨Flatten Image.

This step fuses your blurred background layer to the original image layer.

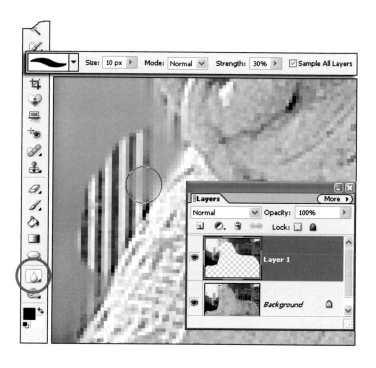

Before

After

Steady the Camera, Sharpen the Shot

A programmer friend shared with me an acronym her department used to classify a particular "computer" error: PEBKAC (Problem Exists Between Keyboard and Chair). At the risk of sounding equally snarky, I must nonetheless tell you that user error, not camera malfunction, also causes most focus problems. The number-one mistake? Not keeping the camera still during the exposure. I don't have an acronym worked out yet, but I'm thinking of something more positive — Steady Camera Avoids Blur? Uh, wait, no. . . .

At any rate, when your entire picture is blurry, camera shake is the most likely cause. In fact, if you're shooting a stationary object like the monument in the Before image, camera shake is the *only* possible cause. Use these strategies to avoid the problem:

❶ When hand-holding the camera, use the proper shooting posture.

I cringe every time I see people using the camera monitor, rather than the viewfinder, to frame their photos. Why? Because when the arms are extended from the body, the possibility of camera shake increases. With the viewfinder, you can brace the camera against your face. Tucking your elbows into your sides further steadies the camera.

Unfortunately, many new cameras no longer offer a viewfinder, which means you have no alternative than to use the monitor. Again, just tuck in your elbows to steady the shot as much as possible.

➋ Increase the shutter speed.

The slower the shutter speed, the longer you must keep the camera still. Remember that adjusting shutter speed also affects exposure; see Chapter 2 for details.

For low-light shots like the example image, you likely will need a slower shutter speed than you can hand-hold, however. My exposure, for example, required a shutter speed of half a second, and I can't hand-hold at speeds slower than about 1/50 second. Many cameras display a little "shaky hand" icon like the one you see in the image to the right if the shutter speed drops below what most people can hand-hold successfully.

➌ Turn on image stabilization if your camera offers it.

Also known as *antishake* or *vibration reduction,* this feature can compensate for a small amount of camera movement.

➍ Mount the camera on a tripod or set it on a steady surface.

Of course, the most obvious solution is to use a tripod. In addition to traditional tripods like the Bogen Imaging, Inc., model shown here (www.bogenimaging.com), camera stores now stock several ingenious alternatives. With the Joby gorillapod (www.joby.com), you can secure a camera to just about any object, as illustrated in the top-right image. Photographers who like to travel light might also appreciate The Pod (also available via the Bogen Web site), which enables you to steady the camera on uneven surfaces, as shown in the lower-right image.

Note: Check your camera manual to find out whether the manufacturer recommends turning off image stabilization when you use a tripod.

Courtesy Joby

Courtesy Bogen Imaging, Inc. Courtesy Bogen Imaging, Inc.

Steady the Camera, Sharpen the Shot *(continued)*

⑤ For tripod shots, take advantage of self-timer mode.

Even when you use a tripod, the act of pressing the shutter button can jiggle the camera enough to blur the image slightly when you shoot long exposures. To avoid this possibility, take advantage of your camera's self-timer mode. In this mode, usually indicated by a stylized clock symbol like the one highlighted in the image to the right, you can enjoy hands-free shooting. Some cameras offer a remote control that provides the same function.

Using a tripod in combination with self-timer mode enabled me to capture the sharp After image. Note, though, that even with a tripod, any moving objects — such as the cars and strolling pedestrians at the bottom of my image — remain blurry at slow shutter speeds. The upcoming makeover, "Turn Water Into Mist with a Slow Shutter," shows you how to take advantage of this fact to emphasize motion in your pictures.

Solve Autofocus Miscues

As the introduction to this chapter states, the autofocus systems on digital cameras work remarkably well. But using the wrong autofocus settings or picture-taking techniques can cause problems like the ones you see in the two Before images here. In the left photo, the entire image is seriously out of focus. In the other picture, the wrong area of the scene is in focus. (The foreground flower should be sharp, not the yellow buds in the background.)

Assuming that you've eliminated camera shake as the cause of your focus problem, follow these steps to troubleshoot autofocus blunders:

❶ Lock in focus correctly.

For autofocus to work, you must press the shutter button in two stages. Frame the picture, press and hold the shutter button halfway down, and wait for the camera to signal that the focus has been set. Depending on your camera, you may see a light near the viewfinder or a symbol in the monitor or viewfinder, as shown in the figure to the right. (Where the light or symbol appears depends on the camera.) Some cameras also sound a beep to indicate that the focus is set. When you get the go-ahead, press the shutter button the rest of the way.

Note: This instruction assumes that your camera doesn't offer *continuous autofocus*. In this mode, the camera continually adjusts focus as you move the lens, and you can press the shutter button all the way in one motion. Cameras that offer this feature usually allow you to switch between it and regular autofocus. Although this feature can come in handy when you need to shoot quickly, it doesn't always focus on the right object. For that reason and because continuous autofocus consumes additional battery power, I prefer regular autofocus.

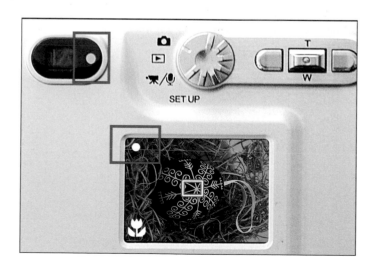

Solve Autofocus Miscues *(continued)*

❷ Check the focus mode.

Some cameras, including the one I used to take the egg image, require you to choose one mode to capture close-ups and another for normal shooting. The close-up, or macro, mode is typically indicated by a flower icon like the one highlighted in the figure here. Check your manual, however, because on some cameras, the macro symbol represents a scene mode that affects both the focus distance and exposure.

Chapter 2 discusses scene modes; for more about macro photography, see the upcoming makeover, "Discover Drama in the Details with Macro-Focusing Power."

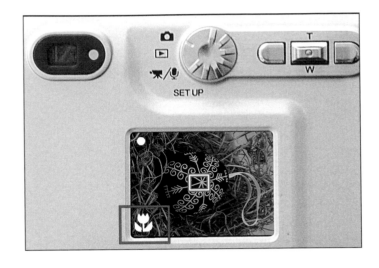

❸ Respect the focus range of your lens.

Every lens has a specific focusing range, which determines the minimum and maximum camera-to-subject distance that you can capture sharply. (Your manual should provide this information.)

The blur in the egg image, for example, occurred because the lens was too close to the subject. To produce the properly focused After image, I simply backed off an inch or so. Naturally, the resulting image contains more background, but I could easily crop away the excess in my photo editor. (Chapter 5 shows you how.)

④ Be sure that your subject is within the autofocus zone.

The *autofocus zone* determines what area of the frame the camera considers when setting focus. In the default setting used on most cameras, focus is based on the distance between the lens and the object that appears at the center of the frame. This mode is sometimes referred to as *center-area* or *center-zone autofocus*. The size and position of the focus zone is usually indicated by a box in the viewfinder or monitor, as illustrated in the image to the right.

If your main subject falls outside the target zone, it may appear blurry, as in my Before flower image. The camera set the focus based on the stem, which is farther from the lens than the white flower. As a result, the stem and other parts of the plant that have the same subject-to-lens distance are sharp, but the white flower is not.

Author Confidential

Troubleshooting Tips for Focus-Free Cameras

If your camera has a *fixed-focus* lens, sometimes referred to as a *focus-free* lens, most of the autofocus troubleshooting tips in this makeover don't apply. With a fixed-focus lens, focus is set at the factory and can't be changed. Typically, the camera is designed to keep in focus any object from a few feet away to infinity. So as long as your subject is within that focusing range and you eliminate any camera shake, your pictures should be sharp. However, some fixed-focus cameras do offer two or three focus settings, each of which produces a different focusing range. For example, many fixed-focus cameras offer a macro setting that enables you to focus at closer distances than the normal setting.

Solve Autofocus Miscues *(continued)*

Note: Although the autofocus zone determines the point of sharpest focus, the sharpness of objects in the rest of the frame depends on their distance from the lens, the aperture setting (f-stop), and the lens focal length. Read the first makeover in this chapter for an explanation.

Advanced cameras often provide additional zone options. In fact, a dizzying array of autofocus schemes exist. But the most popular variations can be loosely grouped into the following categories:

➤ **Selectable zone autofocus:** The photographer can choose from several target zones. For example, a camera might offer a choice of five zones, as illustrated in the figure to the right. You simply select the zone that's closest to the object that you want to use as the focus point.

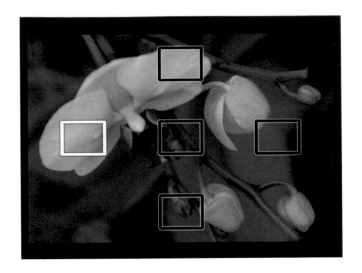

Author Confidential

Faking Out Autofocus

Certain situations stymie even the most capable autofocus system. The following scenes are likely to cause problems: subjects behind a fence or bars; scenes in which there is either very little or a great deal of contrast; objects producing strong reflections; and subjects that feature strong geometric or busy patterns. If you can't get your camera to lock onto your subject, try using a placeholder subject to set focus. Find an object that's about the same distance away as your subject, lock focus on that object (by pressing the shutter button halfway), and then reframe and shoot the picture. Remember, though, that if you're working in autoexposure mode, exposure will also be set when you lock focus. So if your camera offers manual focus, switching to that mode may be a better solution.

➤ **Closest-subject autofocus:** The camera focuses on the object nearest the lens.

➤ **Multispot autofocus:** The camera attempts to choose a focus setting that works for the majority of the objects in the scene.

➤ **Dynamic autofocus:** The camera constantly adjusts focus as needed to keep a moving object sharply focused.

Again, the exact names and functions of these modes vary from camera to camera, so consulting your manual is essential to understanding all your autofocus options.

Don't worry if your camera offers only center-area autofocus, however; you can still focus on any object within the frame. Just frame the shot so that the subject *is* in that center focus zone, and press and hold the shutter button halfway down to lock in focus. Continue to hold that shutter button as you reframe the shot and then press the shutter button the rest of the way.

Julie's Take: Although my camera offers several autofocus options, I prefer to stick with center-area focus and use the frame-press-reframe-press technique if I want to focus on a subject that isn't at the center of the frame. It's one less setting I have to remember to check before I take a picture, and frankly, it's usually faster than resetting the autofocus zone. I took this approach to capture the After image. Now the focus is properly set on the foreground flower, restoring it as the point of visual impact in the photo.

Bring More of the Scene into Focus

The first makeover in this chapter explains how to use shortened depth of field to diminish a busy background and restore emphasis to your main subject. For some subjects, however, you face the opposite challenge: bringing a wider range of the scene into sharp focus. My Before picture of the pair of rhinos is a case in point. The focus is sharp on the foreground animal but too soft on his background companion for my taste.

To extend depth of field, you just take the opposite approach you use to shorten depth of field:

❶ Stop down the aperture.

To *stop down* the aperture means to choose a *higher* f-stop number, which produces a smaller aperture.

Remember that if your camera doesn't offer manual exposure or aperture-priority exposure — meaning you can't specify an exact aperture — you may have access to scene modes that result in different apertures. On most cameras, the Landscape scene mode (usually represented by a mountain-range icon like the one shown to the right) results in the smallest aperture and greatest depth of field.

❷ Zoom out, move back, or both.

Zooming out to a shorter focal length (wider angle view) increases apparent depth of field. Moving farther from your subject also brings more of the scene into focus.

Of course, you have to balance the two options. If you move back so far that you must zoom in to achieve the composition you want, you defeat your purpose.

300mm, f/5.6, 1/160

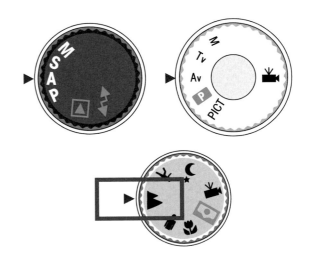

For my rhino image, I wasn't able to zoom out *or* move away significantly; I was one of a crowd of zoo-goers milling around the rhino enclosure, and several heads and a fence would have intruded into the shot had I taken a significantly wider angle or more distant position. Fortunately, zooming out slightly and switching from Portrait to Landscape mode — which stopped down the aperture from f/5.6 to f/7.1 — brought the background rhino into acceptable focus. The After image contains more background, which could easily be cropped to achieve a composition very similar to the zoomed version, without the background blur.

260mm, f/7.1, 1/125

Author Confidential

Sorting Through Focal-Length Confusion

Your camera manual may provide two sets of numbers to describe the focal length of your lens: for example, 5.7mm (35mm equivalent, 37mm). The first value reflects the actual distance between the center of the lens and the image sensor, which is how focal length is measured. But knowing that distance isn't useful for evaluating a digital camera lens because sensor size varies among cameras, and the sensor size determines the area you can capture at a particular focal length. So manufacturers also indicate what the focal length would be on a 35mm film-camera lens, where the size of the recording medium — a 35mm negative — is consistent from model to model. This book states all focal lengths as 35mm film-camera lens equivalents.

Increase Shutter Speed to Freeze Action

You see great action shots in your newspaper every day. But when you try to capture your favorite sports star, Frisbee-catching dog, or bird in flight, your subject appears blurred beyond recognition.

This problem isn't due to a focusing error, but to a too-slow shutter. As an example, I shot the Before picture at a shutter speed of 1/80 second. Although that's less time than it takes to say "cheese," it's nowhere near fast enough to catch a moving subject without blur.

Take these steps to get better results:

① Switch to shutter-priority autoexposure or manual-exposure mode.

In shutter-priority mode, you select the shutter speed, and the camera picks the right aperture to produce a good exposure. Shutter-priority mode is usually indicated by the letters *S* or *Tv* (for *time value*). You also can work in manual-exposure mode and set both shutter speed and aperture yourself.

Alternate Method: If your camera doesn't offer either mode, it may provide an Action mode. In this mode, usually represented by a "running man" icon, the camera automatically selects the highest possible shutter speed. Or, if you have access to aperture-priority mode, try using the lowest f-stop number, which opens the aperture and forces a faster shutter.

② Raise the shutter speed as needed.

The right shutter speed depends on the pace of your subject, so some experimentation is required. For my hockey-star nephew, a speed of 1/160 second wasn't quite fast enough; bumping the speed up to 1/250 second did the trick.

1/80 second

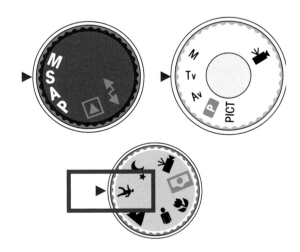

Obviously, my advice to experiment presumes that the subject is willing to repeat the action until you find the ideal shutter speed. If you need to make a quicker decision, a shutter speed of 1/500 second should be safe for all but the fastest subjects — a race car zooming for the checkered flag, for example.

Note: Remember that when you increase shutter speed, you must adjust aperture or ISO setting to maintain the proper exposure. For details, see Chapter 2.

❸ Lock in focus and exposure in advance to compensate for shutter lag.

After you press the shutter button, the camera takes a little time to capture the image. This delay, known as *shutter lag,* can hamper your efforts to catch a moving subject. Adding to the problem, you can't snap another picture until the camera writes the image data to your camera. To cope, try these strategies:

➤ Set focus and exposure ahead of time. If you're working in automatic mode, press and hold the shutter button halfway. When the action occurs, push the button the rest of the way.

➤ To reduce post-capture wait times, turn off the camera's instant-playback feature and shoot without a flash if possible. You can't take a picture while the playback is active or the flash is recycling.

➤ Find out whether your camera can take advantage of high-speed memory cards. If so, using them can reduce image-recording times.

1/160 second

1/250 second

After

Turn Water into Mist with a Slow Shutter

Most subjects that incorporate a moving object call for a fast shutter so the subject appears in sharp focus, as in the preceding makeover. But on occasion, using a shutter speed slow enough to allow the motion to blur adds drama to the scene.

The waterfall image to the right is case in point. I used a shutter speed of 1/40 second, which produced just a little blurring of the water as it cascaded over the rocks. The result is pretty enough, I suppose, but it's nothing special.

To give the photo another dimension, I increased the exposure time, which blurred the water into the soft, romantic mist you see in the After version. Here's how to achieve the look:

① Put your camera on a tripod or other steady surface.

A misty waterfall requires a long exposure — a slow shutter, in other words. And if the camera isn't absolutely still the entire time the shutter is open, the background will be blurred along with the waterfall.

② Set your camera to manual or shutter-priority exposure mode.

If your camera doesn't offer either mode, look for a nighttime exposure mode. Often represented by a moon-and-stars icon, this mode sets the camera to a slower-than-normal exposure. Some cameras enable the flash automatically in that mode; experiment shooting with and without a flash.

1/40 second

Before

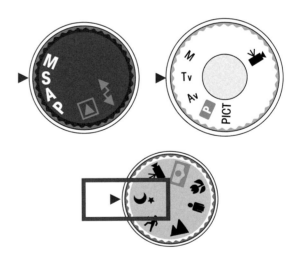

Alternate Method: If you have access to aperture-priority mode but not shutter-priority mode, set the aperture to its smallest setting (highest f-stop). The camera then chooses a slower shutter to compensate.

❸ Experiment with shutter speed until you get the amount of water blur you like.

Shoot the scene at several different speeds — *bracket the exposure,* in photo terms. And don't delete any of your images until you can review them on your computer monitor; the strength of the mist effect is difficult to evaluate on the camera monitor.

Note: In very strong sunshine, a very slow shutter can result in an overexposed image because the camera can't shut down the aperture enough to compensate for all the light that's hitting the image sensor. Professionals solve this problem by using a *neutral density* filter. The filter acts like sunglasses for your lens, only it doesn't alter colors or have a polarizing effect. In fact, in a pinch, you sometimes can get away with putting your sunglasses in front of your lens!

For my After waterfall image, I set the shutter speed to 1/5 second. In addition to increasing the visual interest of the waterfall, the slower shutter helps the composition hold together better. In the Before image, the flowers and the waterfall in the lower-right corner compete for attention. In the After image, the stream of water in the middle becomes more apparent and serves to tie the flower and lower waterfall together. The eye is then drawn all the way from one corner of the image to the other.

1/5 second

Discover Drama in the Details with Macro-Focusing Power

In the earlier makeover, "Solve Autofocus Miscues," the Before egg image illustrates one problem inherent in most cameras: You can get only so close to your subject before the lens loses its ability to focus. I shoot with a professional digital SLR and a pretty decent lens, for example, and yet I could focus no closer to the pocket watch than shown in the Before image to the right.

This limitation in close-up focusing — *macro focusing,* in technical terms — stems from lens economics. If manufacturers were to use lenses that offered super-close focusing as well as good medium and distance-range focusing, camera prices would soar. And because few people would buy cameras that could shoot only close-ups . . . well, you get the idea.

If your attempts at close-up photography leave you frustrated, you can take a couple of steps to improve your macro-focusing power:

Before

❶ Switch to macro-focusing mode if your camera offers it.

On some cameras, you must switch to this mode to take advantage of the maximum close-focusing range of the lens. Look for the flower icon, which has become the universal symbol for macro mode.

❷ If you have a zoom lens, zoom to the recommended focal length.

Consult your manual for this information. On some lenses, you get closer focusing by zooming out to the shortest focal length (wide-angle setting). But with some lenses, you enable macro focusing by zooming in to the maximum focal length.

➌ Buy a set of close-up diopters for even greater macro power.

If you want to get closer than your camera lens allows, the least expensive route is to buy a set of close-up filters, or *diopters*. You simply screw the filter onto the end of your lens. (Your lens must have threads or an adapter that accepts accessory filters.) Usually, the filters come in sets of three or four, with each filter offering a specific magnification power — +1, +2, +4, and so on. You can use a single filter or stack multiple filters to gain their combined macro power, as illustrated in the After image.

Julie's Take: The biggest drawback to diopters is that most produce an extremely shallow depth of field, as these examples show. All these images were shot at an aperture of f/16 — which normally produces a large depth of field — and yet the images are noticeably blurry at the edges. Interchangeable-lens SLR users who do a lot of close-up work may want to invest in a true macro lens, which provides more edge-to-edge sharpness.

One other caveat: Your camera should also offer either a through-the-lens viewfinder or enable you to preview your shot in the camera monitor. With a viewfinder that doesn't offer a through-the-lens view, you can't check focus because the viewfinder can't "see" the diopter over the lens.

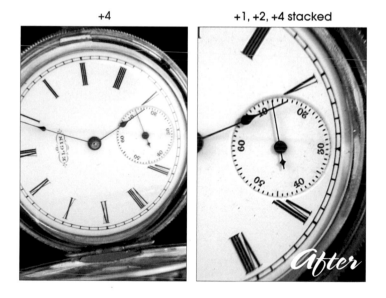

Create the Illusion of Sharper Focus

You often can improve a slightly out-of-focus image like my Before shot of the vintage train by applying a digital process known as *sharpening*. Sharpening doesn't actually alter the focus of your image — it boosts contrast to create the *illusion* of a sharper image.

Many digital cameras offer an in-camera sharpening option. But because an over-sharpened image is very difficult to repair, I suggest that you leave the camera set to the normal sharpening mode and instead sharpen the image as needed in your photo editor. This approach enables you to control exactly how much sharpening is applied and what parts of the image receive the effect.

To get good results, however, you first need to understand how sharpening works. Sharpening filters create light and dark "halos" along so-called *edges* — what most people would call color boundaries. Pixels on the light side of the border get lighter; pixels on the dark side get darker. For example, the images to the right show close-up views of a portion of the train photo. The top close-up is the original image; the lower view has been sharpened. Notice the borders along the white stripe. The light sides of the edges got lighter, and the dark sides got darker.

With that background in mind, you're ready to sharpen. In Elements, the best filter for the job is Unsharp Mask. The filter is named after a darkroom technique that involves using a blurry mask to sharpen an image. (Don't ask.)

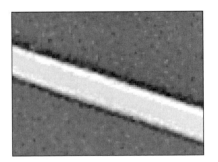

① Make any other changes to your photo, including setting the final print or display size.

Sharpening should always be the last step in your photo-editing process because the amount of sharpening you need depends on the final image colors, contrast, saturation, output size, and resolution.

② Open the Layers palette and duplicate the Background layer.

For reasons that will become clear in Step 9, you should always sharpen on a duplicate layer. So if you don't see the Layers palette, choose Window⇨Layers. Then choose Layer⇨New⇨Layer via Copy to duplicate the Background layer.

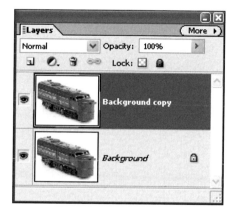

③ Select the area you want to sharpen.

Chapter 1 details three ways to create a selection outline. If you want to apply sharpening to the entire image, as I did for the train image, you can skip this step.

④ Choose Filter⇨Sharpen⇨ Unsharp Mask.

You see the Unsharp Mask dialog box, shown to the right. Select the Preview check box so that you can monitor the results of the filter. To zoom the dialog box preview, click the plus and minus buttons under the preview window.

Start with the Amount, Radius, and Threshold values shown in the figure: 100%, 1.0, and 0, respectively. You should see an immediate sharpening effect.

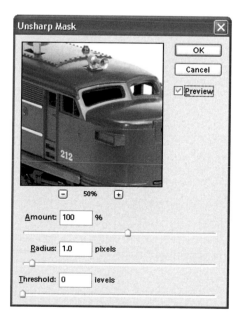

Create the Illusion of Sharper Focus *(continued)*

⑤ Use the Amount slider to adjust the intensity of the effect.

Generally speaking, you don't want to go higher than 150%. At higher values, most images simply take on a rough texture rather than appearing to be more focused.

I set the Amount value for the train image to 130%.

⑥ Adjust the size of the sharpening halos by changing the Radius value.

The Radius option determines the width of the sharpening halos that the filter creates. The higher the number, the wider the halo, as illustrated by the examples to the right.

For most images, somewhere in the 0.5 to 2.0 range is appropriate. A radius value higher than 2.0 can create too-visible halos; a value lower than 0.5 doesn't create much of a sharpening effect at all. Keep in mind that print images typically require more sharpening than on-screen images.

I used a value of 1.5 for the train image, which was destined for print.

⑦ To limit the effect to areas of high contrast, raise the Threshold value.

The Threshold value determines how much difference must exist between neighboring pixels before they are considered an edge and receive the sharpening halos. When the Threshold value is 0, sharpening occurs anywhere there is even the tiniest color shift between neighboring pixels, as shown in the first Threshold example to the right. As you raise the value, the filter is more discriminating, applying sharpening only to strong edges — that is, areas of high contrast, as shown in the second example.

Radius 2.0

Radius 4.0

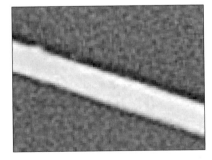

Threshold 0

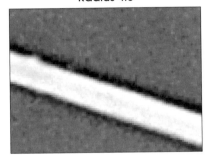

Threshold 10

Julie's Take: Raising the Threshold value slightly is a good idea for portraits and images that contain lots of noise (a defect you can read about in Chapter 1). You then can sharpen the image without adding unwanted texture to skin or making the noise more visible.

For the train image, a Threshold value of 0 created a bit of unwanted texture in the solid blue areas of the train, so I raised the value to 2.

❽ Click OK to close the dialog box and apply the filter.

If you're happy with your results, skip to Step 11. Otherwise, move on to Step 9 to refine the effect.

The image to the right shows you my sharpened train image. The picture is improved, but it needs one final tweak. Close inspection of the image revealed that the sharpening created some unwanted noise and too-obvious sharpening halos along the bottom of the train, as shown in the close-up view.

Note: Be sure to evaluate sharpening by viewing your image at the size it will be printed or displayed on-screen. For print sharpening, do a test print on the intended paper; the texture and gloss of the paper greatly affect how much sharpening you need.

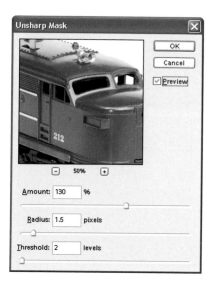

Create the Illusion of Sharper Focus *(continued)*

9 **To reduce the image's overall sharpening impact, lower the Opacity value in the Layers palette.**

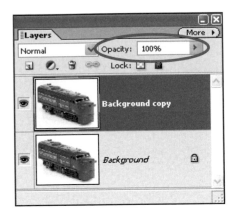

Circled in the figure to the right, the Opacity value determines whether your sharpened layer completely obscures your original image — contained on the Background layer. At any value other than 100%, some of the original pixels remain visible, which lessens the impact of your sharpening application.

10 **To remove sharpening entirely from certain areas, use the Eraser tool on the sharpened layer.**

Select the Eraser tool, circled to the right, and set the tool Mode to Brush. Then drag over the areas where you want to remove the sharpening.

If you set the Opacity value on the options bar to 100%, you completely erase the effect. To partially remove the effect, lower the Opacity value on the options bar. The lower the value, the less you erase with each swipe of the tool. (The options bar Opacity value affects your next tool stroke; the Layers palette Opacity value affects all pixels on the layer.)

In my image, I set the Eraser tool to 50% opacity and erased along the bottom edge of the train, as shown in the figure. This Opacity value enabled me to get rid of the most obvious halos without creating a noticeable break between the sharpened and unsharpened areas.

⓫ When you're satisfied, choose Layer⇨Flatten Image.

This step fuses the sharpened and original layer together.

⓬ Save the sharpened image under a new name.

Why not just overwrite the original image file? Because if you one day need the photo at a different size or resolution, the amount of sharpening you just applied may not be appropriate. So always retain a copy of your original, unsharpened photo.

Before

After

4 COLOR MAKEOVERS

Do you remember learning in your middle-school science class about how the human eye sees color? Inside your eyeballs, you have three receptors, each assigned with the task of discerning one of the three primary colors of light: red, green, and blue. The receptors report the three light values to your brain, which translates those values into color.

Digital cameras capture color by using the exact same concept. Chips on the image sensor record the red, green, and blue light values, which are processed into color by software in the camera.

Even though the science behind your eyes matches digital-imaging technology, you and your camera may not always agree on how colors in an image should appear. Just as two people often perceive a color differently, your camera may produce colors that you think are too warm, too cool, too saturated, or too faded.

This chapter shows you what to do when you're unhappy with the colors your camera delivers. You can find out how to add or remove a color cast, cope with the varying colors of light, and adjust overall color balance. To complete the color discussion, makeovers at the end of the chapter show you how to convert a color image to a black-and-white or sepia-toned photo and also how to deal with a color problem that crops up routinely in flash photos: that infamous portrait-wrecker known as red eye.

Neutralize Light with Manual White Balancing

Every light source has a particular *color temperature,* which simply means that it emits a particular hue. Fluorescent light has a greenish tint, for example, and candlelight has a reddish hue. Color temperature is measured on the Kelvin scale, shown at right.

The human eye compensates for color temperature; people perceive freshly fallen snow as white no matter what the light, for example. A digital camera, however, needs a *white-balance* control to account for these varying colors of light. Without white balancing, an image would take on whatever color cast was produced by the light source.

Most cameras offer both automatic and manual white balancing. Automatic works well in most cases, but when a scene is illuminated by multiple types of light, the white-balance mechanism can make the wrong call. When shooting the jewelry still life shown here, for example, I used tungsten studio lights. But the camera got confused because a nearby window allowed a fair amount of bright sunshine into the room. As a result, the camera warmed the scene too much, giving the image a yellowish color cast.

To remedy a white-balance miscue, take these steps:

① Set your camera to manual white balancing.

The control is usually abbreviated as WB. Some cameras offer a button that takes you directly to the white-balance control; on other models, you must dig through a few menus to change the setting, as shown here.

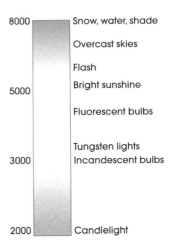

8000	Snow, water, shade
	Overcast skies
	Flash
	Bright sunshine
5000	
	Fluorescent bulbs
	Tungsten lights
3000	Incandescent bulbs
2000	Candlelight

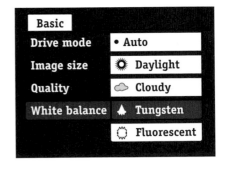

② Select the setting that most closely matches the dominant light source.

I switched my control to Tungsten. The camera then applied a more appropriate color-temperature compensation, resulting in the neutral jewelry shot to the right.

Fortunately, you don't need to memorize the Kelvin scale to know that you've made a good choice; the camera monitor shows you how the white-balance setting affects your image colors.

③ If your camera offers advanced white-balance control, fine-tune the setting if needed.

My digital SLR, for example, enables me to bump the white-balance setting up or down in small increments. Switching to Tungsten +2 produced a slightly cooler image; dialing down to Tungsten –2 produced a slightly warmer image, which I liked best.

Note: When photographers speak of "cooler" and "warmer" images, they're refer-ring to color tones rather than to Kelvin temperatures. A warm image has a red-yellow emphasis, and a cool image leans toward the bluish side.

④ Remove any remaining color cast by using your photo editor's color-adjustment tools.

For how-to's, see the upcoming makeovers "Tweak Color Balance in Your Photo Editor" and "Remove a Color Cast with a Single Click."

Tungsten

Tungsten +2

Tungsten –2

Add Warmth for Better Portraits

If you compare a professional portrait with one taken by an amateur photographer, you may notice a consistent difference: Skin tones in professional portraits tend to have a flattering warm glow, as if the subject just enjoyed a nice tropical holiday.

You, too, can give your subjects a warmer complexion — and without insisting that they visit the tanning booth or glob on tons of dark makeup. All the following techniques will infuse your images with a subtle golden tint:

❶ Add a warming filter to your lens.

A warming filter is simply a colored filter that you put over your camera lens. You can buy warming filters to fit almost any digital SLR lens; look for something called an 81 series filter. (The number indicates the filter color.) If you have a point-and-shoot camera, your lens must have screw threads that accept accessory lenses. In some cases, you may need an adapter to join the lens and filter. Also note that if your camera doesn't offer a through-the-lens viewfinder, you can preview the warming effect only in the camera monitor; the viewfinder can't "see" the filter.

Warming filters come in different strengths, typically indicated by a letter. I shot the first After portrait with an 81B warming filter, shown here. As you can see, this filter strength adds just a subtle amount of warming.

Keep in mind that when you add a warming filter — or almost any color filter — you reduce the amount of light that reaches the image sensor. That means that you need to adjust the exposure accordingly.

Before

After

② Adjust the white-balance setting.

Depending on the light, you may be able to significantly warm an image by using a different white-balance setting. You need to select a white-balance setting for a light source near the top of the Kelvin chart featured in the preceding makeover: Cloudy, Shade, Flash, and so on.

This trick works only if the actual light is farther down the scale than the setting you choose, however. For example, I took the portrait to the right in bright daylight but used the Cloudy white-balance setting. Had I actually taken the picture in cloudy light, there would have been no warming effect.

③ Apply a virtual warming filter in your photo editor.

You can use a color-balancing tool like the Color Variations filter, which I explain in the next makeover. Or, in Elements, take advantage of the more efficient Photo Filter tool.

Choose Filter⇨Adjustments⇨Photo Filter to display the Photo Filter dialog box. Make a selection from the Filter drop-down list. (Select the Preview check box so that you can see the filter effect in the image window.) Drag the Density slider to adjust the amount of color change.

In most cases, selecting the Preserve Luminosity check box works best, but experiment to be sure. If none of the options in the Filters list does the job, click the Color swatch to open the Color Picker and choose a custom color for your filter.

I created my last After image by applying the filter settings shown in the dialog box.

Tweak Color Balance in Your Photo Editor

The Elements Photo Filter tool featured in the preceding makeover has one limitation: It affects the entire tonal range of your image — shadows, highlights, and midtones — as well as all colors. You can't warm blue midtones, for example, without also altering green shadows.

For more control, check your photo editor's menus for a *color-balancing* filter. With this type of filter, you can manipulate three color-range pairs: cyans and reds; magentas and greens; and yellows and blues. And in most programs, you can adjust shadows, midtones, and highlights separately, which is just what I wanted to do to my fall river scene. To my eye, the highlights and shadows are pretty heavy in the cyans and blues, but the midtones are only slightly off in that direction.

In Elements, the tool for the job is called the Color Variations filter; in other programs, it may be named Color Balance, Color Correct, or something similar. Regardless of the name, color-balancing tools are based on the 360-degree color wheel shown to the right. As you add more of one color, you decrease the amount of the color at the opposite position on the wheel. For example, when you add red, you decrease cyan; when you decrease red, you add cyan.

Follow these steps to apply the Elements Variations filter:

❶ Select the part of the image that you want to alter.

Chapter 1 offers an introductory course in selecting. If the entire image needs help, skip this step, as I did for my Before image.

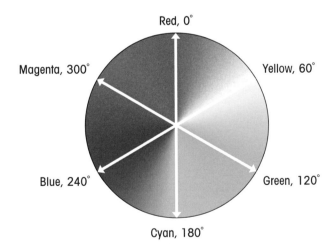

Red, 0°
Magenta, 300°
Yellow, 60°
Blue, 240°
Green, 120°
Cyan, 180°

➋ Choose Enhance⇨ Adjust Color⇨Color Variations.

The Color Variations dialog box appears, as shown to the right. Before and After thumbnails appear at the top of the dialog box so that you can see how your changes will affect the image colors.

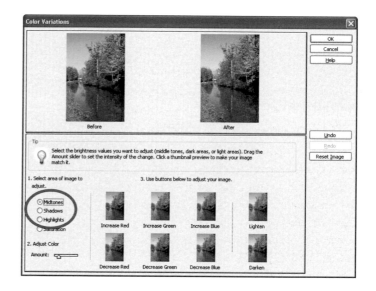

➌ Select the brightness range you want to adjust.

Again, you can tweak shadows, highlights, and midtones separately. Select the option button that corresponds to the range you want to correct first. Assuming that all three ranges need work, I usually start with the midtones.

Ignore the Saturation button. It enables you to adjust color saturation, but this job is best handled with the Hue/Saturation filter, which I discuss later in this chapter. Also ignore the Lighten and Darken thumbnails on the right side of the dialog box and instead use the Levels filter to adjust image exposure, as I explain in Chapter 2.

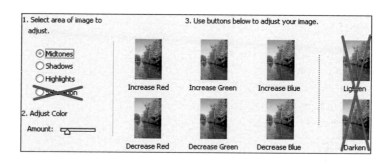

➍ Use the six center thumbnails to balance the colors in the image.

Click any of the Increase thumbnails to add more of that color and subtract its opposite on the color wheel. Click the Decrease thumbnails to reduce the amount of the specified color and increase its opposite.

The dialog box is a little confusing in that you get Increase and Decrease thumbnails only for Red, Green, and Blue. To adjust cyans, yellows, or magentas, just remember the color wheel:

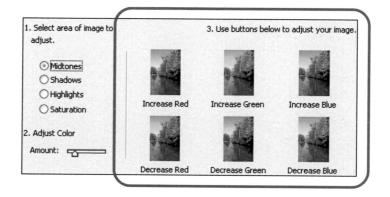

Tweak Color Balance in Your Photo Editor *(continued)*

➤ To add cyan, click Decrease Red; to decrease cyan, click Increase Red.

➤ To add yellow, click Decrease Blue; to reduce yellow, click Increase Blue.

➤ To add magenta, click Decrease Green; to reduce magenta, click Increase Green.

❺ Control the degree of shift by adjusting the Amount slider.

If you want your next thumbnail click to produce a greater change, drag the Amount slider to the right. To produce a more subtle change, drag the slider left.

Any time a thumbnail click shifts colors too far in one direction, just click the Undo button on the right side of the dialog box, adjust the Amount slider, and try again.

❻ Repeat Steps 3 through 5 for the other two brightness ranges.

To fix my image, I set the Amount slider at the position shown in the dialog box here. For the midtones, I clicked once on Increase Red and once on Decrease Blue, which in turn decreased cyan and increased yellow.

For the shadows and highlights, I clicked three times on the Increase Red and Decrease Blue thumbnails. Now the golden autumn tones become the color focus of the image rather than the sky. The leaves reflected in the water are much more visible, as well.

❼ When you're happy with the image colors, click OK.

Elements applies your changes and closes the dialog box.

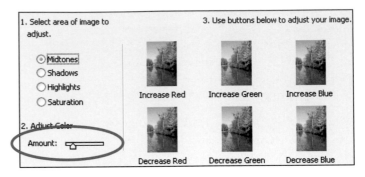

Before

After

Remove a Color Cast with a Single Click

Don't worry too much if you can't achieve a perfectly neutral image by tweaking your camera's white-balance setting. Every photo-editing program offers some sort of tool that enables you to easily remove any unwanted color cast.

In Photoshop Elements, this tool is called Remove Color Cast, and it works like so:

❶ Choose Enhance⇨ Adjust Color⇨Remove Color Cast.

You see the Remove Color Cast dialog box shown to the right.

❷ Click an object in your image that should be white, gray, or black.

Elements scratches its head and figures out how to adjust the image so that the color cast is removed.

Don't like the results? Click the Reset button in the dialog box and try again. (The button becomes available after your first click in the image.)

For my too-blue turtle image, I clicked the border around the eye, which I knew should be a light gray.

❸ Click OK to close the dialog box.

If you can't find the right spot to click to neutralize your image, try using the Color Variations filter, which I describe in the preceding makeover, to do the job.

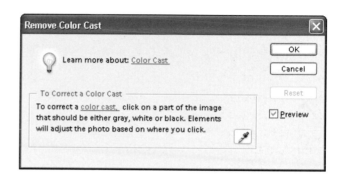

Dial Back Saturation to Reveal Subtle Details

If you dig through your camera menus, you'll probably find a setting that enables you to adjust color saturation. *Saturation* refers to the intensity or purity of a color. A fully saturated color is a pure hue that contains no black, gray, or white.

Most people's natural inclination is to go for broke when it comes to saturation. Human eyes are naturally attracted to bold, vibrant colors, so why not crank up the color machine all the way?

Well, as the Before picture illustrates, too much saturation is actually a bad thing. When you max out saturation, colors that should contain subtle amounts of black or white shift to the pure hue, which eradicates shadow and highlight detail.

In addition, oversaturated images often suffer from *color blooming* — a defect that creates weird color halos like the ones you see in the close-up in the Before images to the right. Notice especially the magenta halos along the edges of the blue areas of the bowl.

To avoid oversaturation problems, take these steps:

❶ Set your camera's saturation control to Normal.

Check your manual — the setting that results in normal saturation may be called something different.

Take some test shots at every saturation setting, too, because the impact of different settings varies depending on the camera.

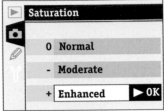

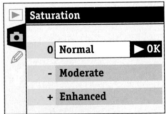

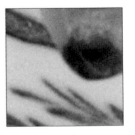

② If needed, increase saturation slightly in your photo editor.

In Elements, choose Enhance⟹Adjust Color⟹Adjust Hue/Saturation to display the dialog box shown to the right.

To increase the saturation of all colors in the image, select Master from the Edit drop-down list, and then drag the Saturation slider to the right. You also can adjust an individual color range by selecting it from the Edit list, as shown here.

For my image, I boosted saturation only for the yellows and reds and left the other color ranges (magenta, green, blue, and cyan) alone. Now the flower has more "pop," and the blue background no longer overwhelms the image.

Click OK to close the dialog box when you're satisfied with your changes.

③ When printing, test different density settings.

Most printers enable you to adjust the density of the ink (or dye or toner), which in turn affects the saturation of printed colors. If the density is too high, you can cause the same problem as a high saturation setting in your camera: Colors that should be slightly desaturated appear full strength, resulting in more loss of detail. In addition, high density ink application can cause colors to bleed together on certain papers.

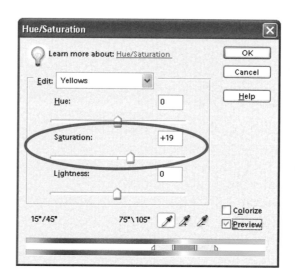

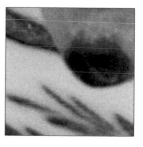

Direct the Eye with Color

Sometimes, a color choice that looks great through the viewfinder turns out to be a mistake when you see the resulting image. Such was the case with this floral still life. When I shot the scene, the orange silk that I used for the tablecloth and the green curtain behind seemed an ideal stage for the flowers. But when I later looked at the picture on my computer monitor, it was immediately apparent that the silk was too vibrant, drawing attention away from the flowers, and the curtain didn't provide enough contrast to the green parts of the arrangement.

If you don't have the time or opportunity to reshoot your photo, you can fix the problem in your photo editor. Follow these steps to tone down the distracting objects and redirect the eye to your main subject:

❶ Select the object you want to alter.

Chapter 1 offers an introduction to selecting. For this image, I used the Magic Wand to select the tablecloth and the curtain, taking care to select all the curtain areas peeking through the floral arrangement.

❷ Choose Enhance⇨ Adjust Color⇨Adjust Hue/ Saturation.

You see the Hue/Saturation dialog box, shown to the right.

❸ Select Master from the Edit drop-down list.

This instruction assumes that you want to desaturate all colors in the distracting object.

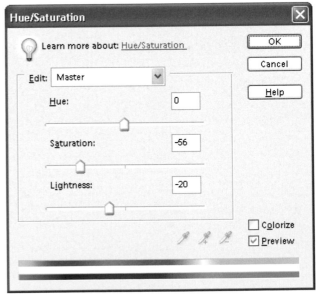

If not, you can select any of six color ranges from the drop-down list.

④ Drag the Saturation slider to the left.

Select the Preview check box so that you can see the change in the image window.

⑤ If needed, also adjust the Lightness slider.

I dragged the Lightness slider a little to the left to reduce the brightness of the selected areas. (Do *not* use this control to adjust overall image exposure; it reduces tonal range.)

⑥ Click OK.

My After image appears to the right. The flowers now take the main stage, no longer fighting with the backdrop for attention.

Author Confidential

Keep Photos from Fading

Although an oversaturated image is a problem, no one likes a dull, faded picture, either. To keep digital prints from losing their color, store them in archival boxes or albums or frame them behind glass, using acid-free matte board. Avoid displaying photos in areas that receive lots of light (particularly direct sunlight), and prevent exposure to humidity and environmental pollutants. If you're printing your own photos, understand that color fidelity depends on both the paper and the ink, dye, or toner you use. To read more about print longevity, visit www.wilhelm-imaging.com, the Web site of a leading expert in the subject.

Lower the Odds of Red Eye

Red eye — that photographic phenomenon that makes a person's eyes appear to emit a red glow — is a common problem with photos taken indoors with a flash.

To reduce the occurrence of red eye, it helps to understand exactly why it happens in the first place. When a flash is aimed directly at the eyes, the retina of the eye can reflect the light back toward the camera lens. That reflection picks up the red in the blood vessels, and the result is a red glint. In animal eyes, there is a colored coating behind the retina, so the reflected light usually gives the eyes a yellow, white, or green glow instead of red.

With that little science lesson out of the way, the following strategies help reduce the possibility of red eye:

❶ Brighten the room as much as possible.

As you do, your subject's pupils narrow in response, so less light from the flash makes it to that reflective retina. (Now you know why red eye rarely occurs when you shoot with a flash outdoors.) You can even ask your subjects to look directly at a lamp for a few seconds before you snap the picture.

❷ Switch the flash to red-eye-reduction mode.

In this mode, usually indicated by a flash symbol together with an eyeball, as shown here, the flash emits a little pre-flash before the actual flash fires and the shot is captured. The idea is the same as turning up the ambient room light: to stop down the pupils. Be sure to warn your subjects that

they will see two flashes, though. Otherwise, they may assume that the picture has been captured after the first flash and look away.

❸ If you use an external flash, aim the flash above the subject.

With this positioning, the flash won't fire directly into the subject's eyes but instead will bounce off the nearest wall or ceiling. See Chapter 2 for tips on how to shoot portraits indoors without using a flash at all.

❹ Compose the photo so that the subject doesn't look directly at the lens or flash.

Such poses eliminate or reduce the chance of red eye. I took this approach for the second shot of my nephew and his dog, for example. Notice that the dog is looking at an angle that does create a problem for her eyes, but the boy is not. (And no, you aren't crazy — this is a different dog from the first image. Dog number one got bored with posing, so we had to bring in his sister.)

❺ If all else fails, remove red eye in your photo editor.

The next makeover shows you how. Some cameras even offer an automated red-eye remover that takes care of the problem right in the camera; usually, you access it via the playback menu. On some models, this feature works well, but I don't advise using it unless the camera allows you to review the repair before overwriting your original file. Automated red-eye removal sometimes misses its target and instead places an unnatural blob of color at the wrong position on the eye.

Repair Red Eye (Or Green, Yellow, or White Eye)

Despite your best efforts, you're bound to wind up with red-eye problems occasionally. Fortunately, repairing the defect in a photo editor is pretty easy. Here's how:

❶ Try your program's automated red-eye removal tool.

Most every photo editing program offers one; some work better than others.

In Elements, select the Red-Eye Removal tool, shown circled in the figure to the right. Set both options bar controls to 50%, and then drag to enclose the eyeball in a rectangular box, as shown to the right. When you release the mouse button, the program analyzes the area inside the box and attempts to repair what it perceives as the red-eye areas.

The Elements red-eye tool does the job most of the time. But it sometimes leaves some stray red pixels behind, as it did for my sample photo. Experiment with changing the options bar settings and dragging again once or twice.

❷ If you don't get good results after a few tries, move on.

In my image, I couldn't get rid of all the red despite several tries. The Red-Eye Removal tool consistently missed the red pixels along the upper part of the pupil, as shown to the right. If your image is similarly resistant, don't waste any more time fooling around with the automated tool; no matter how sophisticated, it just isn't going to work on all cases of red eye. Instead, follow the remaining steps to fix the area "manually."

Before

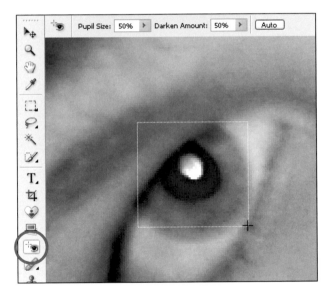

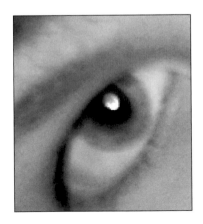

❸ Create a new image layer.

Display the Layers palette, shown here, by choosing Window⇨Layers. Click the New Layer icon, circled in the figure, to create a new, empty layer. In Step 7, you paint in new eye pixels on this layer.

❹ Set the layer-blending mode to Color.

The blending-mode control, located just above the New Layer icon in the Layers palette, adjusts how the pixels on one layer mix with those on the layer below. In the Color mode, Elements uses the color of pixels on the top layer but retains the shadows and highlights of the bottom layer. This arrangement is perfect for red-eye repair because it changes the color of the red pixels but retains the natural shading in the eyeball.

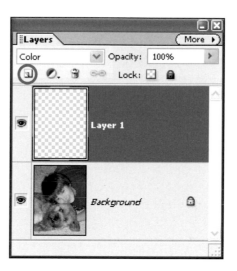

❺ Select the Brush tool.

Set the options bar controls as shown here. Work with a small brush, and set the brush Hardness value to about 90%. (See Chapter 1 if you need help with setting brush options.)

❻ Set the foreground paint color to match the eye color you want.

Chapter 1 also shows you how to select paint colors. For quick results, select the Eyedropper tool and click on a pupil pixel that wasn't affected by red eye, if any exist.

❼ Paint over the red pixels.

As you paint, you may need to adjust the paint color periodically to get natural results. Notice that your paint has no effect on any pixels that are fully white or black. This happens because of the layer-blending mode (Color), which leaves white and black pixels unchanged.

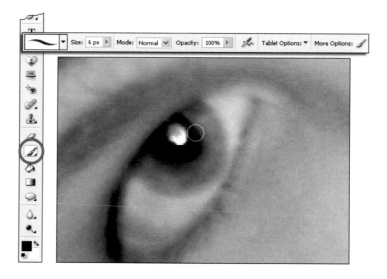

Repair Red Eye (Or Green, Yellow, or White Eye) *(continued)*

The only problem with this technique is that it doesn't work if the problem areas are extremely bright, which is the case with the dog's eyes. Again, this is a function of the Color blending mode. Even if you paint with absolute black, your repaired eyeball will appear light gray, as you see in the left dog eye here. If you aren't able to repair the entire eye with this technique, move on to the next step. Otherwise, skip to Step 9.

⑧ To fix remaining areas, paint on another new layer in the Normal mode.

Just click that New Layer icon in the Layers palette to create a second empty layer (see the figure to the right). This time, however, set the layer blending mode to Normal.

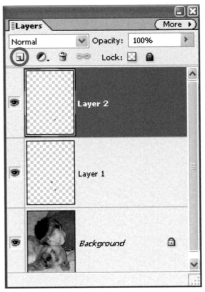

At this point, I'd like to offer you some other magical fix, but unfortunately, there isn't one. The only solution is to take your time and re-create a realistic eye with paint. You'll need to paint in your own shadows, highlights, and midtones, because your paint pixels will obscure the original ones. Don't forget to leave a few pixels completely white to re-create the natural specular highlights that occur in the eye. If you're unfamiliar with how a pupil looks, refer to an existing picture in which your subject doesn't have the red/white/green/yellow eye problem.

⑨ Choose Layer⇨Flatten Image.

This step merges your newly painted eye layers with the original image.

Add Impact by Going Gray

Most people are drawn to photos that feature bold, eye-popping color. But sometimes, color can actually be a negative element. This family portrait is a case in point. In the Before image, the brightly colored clothing and background distract the eye from the faces.

When you don't have the opportunity to tone down the colors in a scene, experiment with creating a *grayscale* picture. A grayscale image contains just black, white, and shades of gray. In other words, it's what most people refer to as a *black-and-white* photograph. (Technically, a black-and-white image contains only black and white.)

Most digital cameras provide a color-effects setting that enables you to shoot black-and-white pictures. However, I suggest that you instead capture a full-color image and then use your photo editor to produce your grayscale version. You can easily convert a color image to grayscale, but the reverse isn't true.

Going gray requires only two steps in Photoshop Elements:

❶ Choose Image⇨Mode⇨Grayscale.

Elements sucks all the color out of your image and converts it from the RGB color mode (the standard full-color mode) to the Grayscale mode.

Alternate Method: In Grayscale mode, pictures may contain only black, white, and shades of gray. If you plan to add color to the image later — for example, to add

colored text — do your conversion via a different command: Enhance⇨Adjust Color⇨ Remove Color. With this command, the image turns gray but remains in the RGB mode. Don't confuse this command with the Remove Color Cast command, which is explained in the earlier makeover, "Remove a Color Cast with a Single Click."

② Save your black-and-white image under a new name.

You may want the original colors back some day. So save the black-and-white version under a new name so that you can retain both a color and black-and-white copy.

Give Your Picture an Antique Look

Many digital cameras not only can capture black-and-white images, but also can produce *sepia-toned* images. A sepia-toned photograph looks like an old black-and-white picture that has acquired a brownish-yellow tint over time.

Going the sepia route is another good solution for dealing with color elements that distract from the compositional focus of your image. But as with black-and-white pictures, I suggest that you don't capture your images in the sepia mode but instead shoot in full-color mode and then convert to sepia in your photo editor. Again, you can always convert a color picture to either black-and-white or sepia, but you can't go the other direction.

Doing the conversion in your photo editor also gives you more control over the color and intensity of the sepia tint you add. And most photo editors offer a special-effects filter that makes the conversion a very easy process.

To convert a color image to sepia (or any other tint) in Elements, follow these steps:

1 Choose Enhance⇨ Adjust Color⇨Adjust Hue/ Saturation.

You see the Hue/Saturation dialog box.

2 Select the Colorize and Preview check boxes.

Your photo now appears as a black-and-white image with a translucent tint.

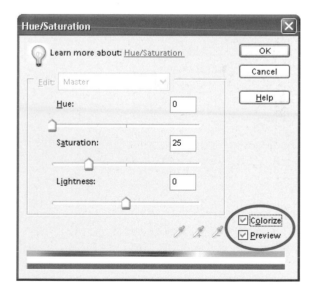

Give Your Picture an Antique Look *(continued)*

**③ Drag the Hue slider
to adjust the tint color.**

I set the slider to the position shown in the
dialog box to produce the sepia version of
my full-color original.

**④ Drag the Saturation slider to
adjust the intensity of the tint.**

By default, the Saturation slider is set to –25.
I increased the Saturation slightly, to –20.
(You don't see the minus sign in the Hue
and Saturation value boxes above the slider,
but any setting to the left of the slider mid-
point produces a negative value.)

Note: Don't use the Lightness slider to
adjust the image brightness and contrast.
Instead, use the more capable Levels filter
(which I discuss in Chapter 2).

**⑤ Save your picture
under a new name.**

That way, you retain your full-color original
in case you need it later. You can see my full-
color original and its sepia-toned version to
the right.

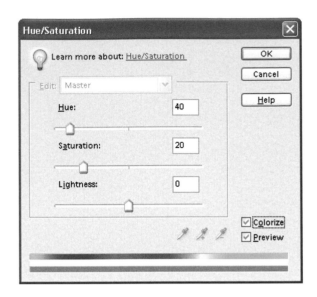

Don't Expect Color Perfection

One of the most commonly heard complaints among digital photographers is that the colors they see on their monitors vary widely from those in their printed images. You can get monitor and printer more in synch by following the Chapter 1 instructions for calibrating and profiling your monitor, which ensures that you're viewing your photos on a neutral canvas. If your photo software supports color management, implementing those features helps as well. (Chapter 1 explains color management, and the appendix shows you how to set up the related features in Photoshop Elements.)

If your colors still remain wildly inconsistent, the problem is most likely due to a clogged print head or depleted ink tank. Your printer manual should tell you how to deal with both problems. Also try printing on paper sold by the printer manufacturer rather than cheap, store-brand paper. The manufacturer's paper is engineered expressly to work with the printer's inks and ink-delivery system.

Even if you take all these steps, however, you shouldn't expect perfect color matching between screen and paper no matter how sophisticated your digital darkroom. The reason is that monitors and printers use two different technologies for reproducing color. A monitor displays color by mixing red, green, and blue light, but a printer creates colors by mixing primary colors of ink: cyan, magenta, yellow, and, usually, black. And unfortunately, it's simply impossible to reproduce with ink all the colors that you can create with light.

5 MORE DIGITAL DARKROOM MAKEOVERS

Photo retouching once was a task attempted only by professionals with specialized experience. But with the advent of digital photography and photo-editing software, all you need to clean up problem pictures is a computer, a few hours of spare time, and a willingness to learn some basic retouching skills.

Retouching techniques related to specific makeovers are scattered throughout earlier chapters. Chapter 2 shows you how to manipulate exposure, for example; Chapter 3 offers tips for tweaking focus; and Chapter 4 discusses color correction. To round out your digital darkroom repertoire, this chapter offers a few additional general-purpose techniques. You can find detailed instructions for straightening a tilting horizon line, correcting converging vertical lines, removing unwanted objects and other blemishes, and more.

Straighten a Tilting Image

Sometimes, a stormy day can produce amazing light. I shot this photo at a moment when the sun broke through an opening in the clouds, for example. I love the contrast between the warm reds and yellows of the buildings and the stormy skies. I'd like the image even more, though, had I not been so enamored by the light that I was sloppy with my camera angle. The horizon line is so tilted that it appears as though the foreground sculpture might roll away.

Fortunately, fixing a tilting horizon is easy:

① Choose Select⇨All.

Your entire image is selected.

② Choose Image⇨Transform⇨ Free Transform.

The options bar offers the controls you see to the right, and a solid outline surrounds your image, with eight little boxes around the perimeter. Those little boxes are officially known as *handles*. (If you don't see the handles, either enlarge the image window or zoom out so that your image doesn't fill the window completely.)

③ Select the Anti-alias check box.

New to Version 4.0, this option smoothes curved and vertical lines when appropriate.

④ Place your cursor outside the outline, near a corner handle.

Your cursor should change into a curved, double-headed arrow cursor. If it doesn't, move it closer to the corner handle.

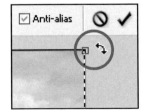

⑤ Drag up or down to rotate the image.

For precise moves, you can also enter a value in the Rotate value box on the options bar, circled in the figure. Double-click the box and then type in the rotation angle. Or, while the box is highlighted, press the up- and down-arrow keys to shift the value by one tenth of a degree.

Should you want to cancel out of the operation for any reason, click the Cancel button on the right end of the options bar (also circled in the figure).

⑥ Click the Accept check mark on the options bar to apply the rotation.

I circled the check mark in the figure to the right.

Notice that in the course of the rotation, a part of your image shifts out of view, leaving portions of the image canvas empty. (The *canvas* is the virtual background upon which every image rests.) The canvas takes on the current background paint color — white, in my example.

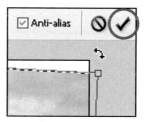

⑦ Crop the image to trim away the empty canvas areas.

Flip ahead to the cropping makeovers later in this chapter to find out how to take this step.

Straighten Converging Verticals

When you shoot with a wide-angle lens, your pictures may exhibit a problem known as *convergence.* Structures that should be vertical appear to lean toward each other, as in the image to the right, or away from each other. Which way your vertical structures lean depends on whether you take the picture with your lens pointed up or down with respect to the structures.

To avoid convergence, you can buy super-expensive specialty lenses, called shift-tilt lenses, that compensate for the problem. Or you can use the following technique to correct convergence in your photo editor.

Note: You do lose some of your original image area in the process, so complete this project before you do any cropping.

❶ Enlarge the image canvas by 25 percent.

Again, the *canvas* is the virtual background on which all images rest in Elements. Normally, your image covers the entire canvas. The convergence-correction process stretches your image slightly, however, and you need to extend the canvas on all four sides to hold the extended image areas.

Choose Image⟹Resize⟹Canvas Size to display the Canvas Size dialog box. Select the Relative check box and set the unit of measurement to Percent. Then enter 25 in the Width and Height boxes. Make sure that the center tile in the Anchor grid circled in the figure is selected; if not, click that tile. Finally, set the Canvas Extension Color option to White and click OK. The blank canvas area appears around your image.

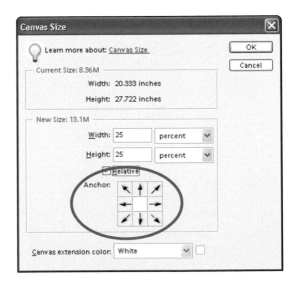

❷ Choose Select⟹All.

The entire image becomes surrounded by a selection outline.

③ Choose Image⇨Transform⇨ Free Transform.

Your image should now appear something like you see in the figure to the right. The image is surrounded by a solid outline that's anchored by eight square handles, and the options bar offers a collection of transformation controls. (Enlarge the image window if you don't see the handles.)

④ Select the Anti-alias check box on the options bar.

This option, new in Version 4.0, smoothes the jagged edges that can occur along curved and diagonal lines.

⑤ In Windows, press Ctrl+Alt+Shift as you drag one of the top corner handles.

On a Mac, press ⌘+Option+Shift as you drag.

If your verticals lean toward the center of the image, as in the example photo, drag the handle outward. If the verticals lean toward the edges of the frame, drag the handle inward.

As you drag one handle, the handle on the opposite corner moves in tandem, producing a perspective shift. Keep dragging until your vertical structures no longer lean. For my example image, I dragged the handles to the position you see in the figure. The convergence correction is most noticeable in building on the far right, just behind the foreground flag pole.

On occasion, you may need to distort one corner of the image more than the other. To do so, Ctrl+drag (Windows) or ⌘+drag (Mac) a corner handle.

Straighten Converging Verticals *(continued)*

After you straighten your leaning verticals, you may notice that the perspective shift has distorted your image a little. If you dragged the corner handles outward, your image looks squashed in height; if you dragged inward, the image appears stretched in height. You fix this problem in the next step.

❻ Drag the top center handle up or down as needed to restore the original proportions of structures in the image.

For the example, I dragged the center handle to the position shown in the figure. This change restores the original size relationships between the structures in the photo.

❼ Click the Accept check mark at the right end of the options bar.

The transformation handles and options bar controls disappear, and you're left with an irregularly shaped image atop your white canvas.

❽ Crop away the empty canvas area.

Follow the instructions on the next few pages to clip away the blank canvas. For composition reasons, I cropped my example image a little more tightly than was necessary; you can see the final results to the right.

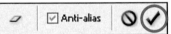

Crop to a Better Composition

On several occasions throughout this book, I encourage you to include a little background in your shots so that you have the flexibility to crop the image to a variety of traditional frame sizes. But if you frame *too* loosely, your subject can get lost in the image.

Sometimes, of course, the limitations of lens or location restrict you from getting closer to your subject, forcing you to include more background than you'd like. Or circumstances may force you to shoot so quickly that you simply don't have time to compose the image perfectly.

Whatever the factors that led to excess background, you have two options for getting rid of it. To crop to a specific frame size, see the next makeover. If you don't care about achieving exact dimensions, follow these steps:

❶ Choose Window⇨Info to display the Info palette.

Displaying the Info palette enables you to monitor the exact size of your Crop boundary, which is important for reasons that become clear in Step 7.

❷ Set the palette unit of measurement to pixels.

To do so, click the More button in the top-right corner of the palette and then choose Palette Options from the pop-up menu. You see the Info Palette Options dialog box, shown to the right. Select Pixels from the Ruler Units drop-down list and then click OK.

Note: If the Info palette obscures your image, drag it out of the way. But position it so that you can see the W (width) and H (height) values in the lower-right corner.

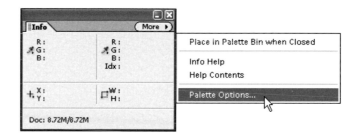

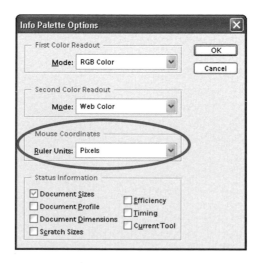

Crop to a Better Composition *(continued)*

❸ Select the Crop tool.

Either click the tool icon, near the middle of the toolbox, or just press C.

❹ Set the options bar controls as shown in the figure.

Specifically, set the Aspect Ratio control to No Restriction and make sure that the Width, Height, and Resolution boxes are empty.

❺ Drag to create an initial cropping boundary.

The boundary appears as a blinking selection outline with square handles around the perimeter. Two buttons appear underneath the outline: a green check mark for accepting the crop boundary and a red cancel button for escaping out of the operation. Areas outside the crop boundary appear dimmed.

❻ Adjust the crop boundary as needed.

To resize the boundary, drag any handle. Drag the side or center handles to adjust the boundary's width or height. Drag a corner handle to adjust width and height together. To move the boundary, drag inside it.

❼ Check the W and H values in the Info palette.

The W (width) value indicates the width of the area inside the crop boundary, in pixels — in other words, the number of remaining horizontal pixels. The H (height) value represents the number of vertical pixels. If you plan to print your picture, be sure that the pixel dimensions are appropriate for size of print you want.

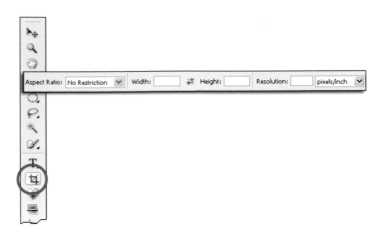

Chapter 1 contains a detailed explanation of this issue, but the short story is that a good print requires at least 200 pixels per linear inch. So dividing the number of horizontal pixels by 200 tells you the maximum width of the print you'll be able to produce; divide the number of vertical pixels by 200 to determine the maximum print height. If you want a bigger print than the numbers in the Info palette suggest, you need to enlarge the crop boundary.

⑧ Click the green Accept check mark or press Enter.

Again, the check mark is underneath the image in version 4.0 (but you must look on the options bar in version 3.0). After you click, anything that was outside the crop boundary is clipped away.

⑨ Save your cropped image under a new name.

You never know: You may want the entire original image back some day. So save the cropped version under a different name.

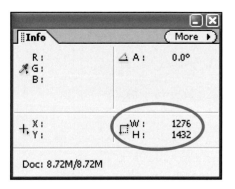

Before

After

Crop to Specific Dimensions

Often, you may want to crop your image so that it conforms to the proportions of a traditional print size — for example, 4 x 6 inches or 5 x 7 inches. (See Chapter 1 for an explanation of why cropping is necessary.) Or you may need a photo that fits a certain hole in a publication layout.

The Elements Crop tool offers a mode that allows you to handle this job. But if you use the tool in this mode, the image print resolution (measured in ppi) is automatically adjusted during the cropping process. I prefer to take care of resolution duties myself and instead use the Crop command to trim my photos to a specific size. (In Elements, use the Image⇨Resize⇨Image Size command to establish print resolution.)

Follow these steps to crop your photo to specific dimensions:

❶ Display the Info palette by choosing Window⇨Info.

Follow Steps 1 and 2 in the preceding makeover to display pixels as the unit of measurement in the palette.

❷ Select the Rectangular Marquee tool.

The tool lives near the top of the toolbox, sharing a flyout menu with the Elliptical Marquee tool.

❸ Set the options bar controls as shown in the first figure.

Set the Feather value to 0 and select Fixed Aspect Ratio from the Mode drop-down list.

❹ Enter the desired image proportions in the Width and Height boxes.

For example, if you want to crop a picture to fit a 4-x-6-inch frame, enter 4 and 6, respectively, into the boxes.

❺ Drag to enclose the area you want to keep in a selection outline.

As you drag, the program limits the tool to selecting an area with the proportions you entered in the Width and Height boxes in Step 4. You can make the outline any size you want; only the proportions (aspect ratio) are restricted.

In the figure to the right, the dotted lines represent my selection outline; the red arrow, the direction of my drag. Anything outside the outline will be cropped away in the next step.

If you don't get the outline right the first time, just click and drag again. To relocate an existing outline, drag inside it. You can also press the arrow keys to nudge the outline into place.

Note: As when you use the Crop tool, monitor the Info palette carefully if you plan to print the image. When a selection outline is active, the W and H values in the palette show the width and height of the outline, respectively, in pixels. Be sure that your selection outline encompasses enough pixels to produce the size of print you want. You need at least 200 pixels for each linear inch of your print. See the Chapter 1 discussion about resolution for more information about pixels and print size.

❻ Choose Image➪Crop.

Elements crops the image, eliminating anything outside the selection outline. My final image to the right is now perfectly sized to fit a 4-x-6-inch frame.

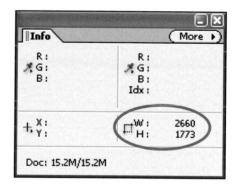

Clone Away Intrusive Objects

You see the perfect scene through your viewfinder. Or rather, it *would* be perfect if not for those telephone wires running through the background . . . or the trash can looming close to your subject . . . or the doofus in the "I'm with stupid" shirt who refuses to move out of the frame.

When a minor flaw mars an otherwise ideal image, press the shutter button anyway. Then open the picture in your photo editor and use the Clone tool to get rid of the problem. With this tool, you can duplicate — *clone* — an unblemished portion of your image and then paste the copies over the bad areas.

The following steps give you the cloning how-to, using the antique tractor image as an example. My mission with this image was to remove the red security cable that runs through the bottom of the image.

Julie's Take: Don't get discouraged if you don't grasp everything on the first or even fifteenth journey through these steps, by the way. The Clone tool is a little confusing, and you may need more than a few practice sessions to fully understand it.

❶ Create a new layer to hold your cloned pixels.

For safety's sake, you should never clone directly on your original image. Instead, put your cloning strokes on a separate layer.

To add a new, empty layer, choose Window➪Layers to display the Layers palette. Then click the New Layer icon, circled in the figure to the right.

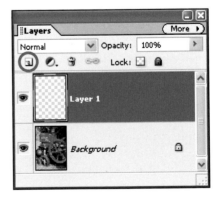

② Select the Clone tool.

Officially, the tool is named the Clone Stamp tool. But I'm going with standard imaging lingo and referring to it simply as the Clone tool.

Whatever you call it, the tool shares a fly-out menu with the Pattern Stamp tool. The two tool icons look very similar, so be sure to click the right one.

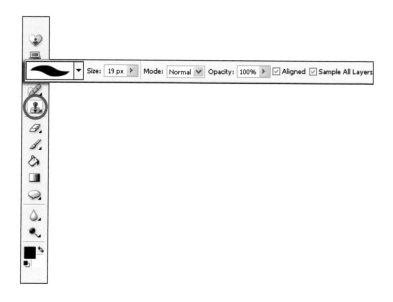

③ Select a brush from the Brushes palette.

Click the brushes palette icon (circled in the second figure) to open the palette. Then click a brush icon in the palette. (Chapter 1 provides more help with this step if you need it.) Generally, a soft brush works better than a hard one for cloning because a hard brush tends to leave noticeable "brush marks" behind.

Note: The Clone tool doesn't provide a Hardness control. You can choose either a fully soft or fully hard brush from the palette. (The fuzzy icons represent soft brushes.) However, you can increase brush hardness by 25 percent by pressing Shift+]. Each press of this key combo adjusts the hardness of your next paint stroke by 25 percent. (You don't need to keep the keys pressed as you use the brush.) To reduce hardness by 25 percent, press Shift+[.

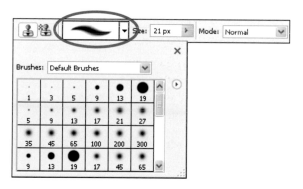

After selecting a brush icon from the palette, you can adjust its diameter by using the Size control on the options bar. The proper size depends on what you're cloning, of course; you may need to adjust it as you work on different areas of the image.

Clone Away Intrusive Objects *(continued)*

④ Set the Mode control to Normal and the Opacity value to 100%.

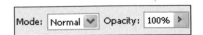

Use these values so that your cloned pixels will completely obscure the original pixels.

⑤ Alt+click (Windows) or Option+click (Mac) to establish the initial clone source.

By *clone source,* I mean the area you want to use to cover up the problem area. When you press and hold Alt or Option, a little target cursor appears to let you know that you're about to set the clone source. Click the spot you want to use as the initial clone source. Then release the Alt/Option key.

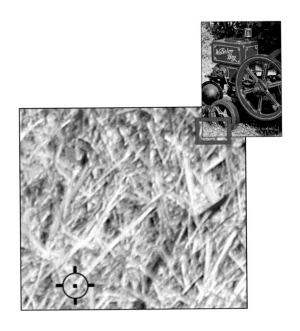

For my sample image, I wanted to cover the cable by cloning some of the surrounding grass over it, so I Alt+clicked in the lower-left corner of the image. The target cursor in the close-up inset shows you the exact location of my initial clone source.

⑥ Use the Aligned option to control whether the tool clones the same pixels each time you click or drag.

My, that's helpful, eh? Here's the deal: After you Alt+click or Option+click and then begin cloning, you see two cursors: a crosshair cursor and a regular brush cursor. The crosshair cursor represents the current clone source; the round cursor represents the Clone tool cursor. (This assumes you set your cursor display to Full Brush Size, as suggested in Chapter 1.)

Clone
source
cursor

Tool
cursor

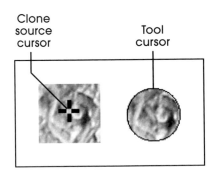

If you click with the Clone tool, the tool picks up one cursor's worth of pixels from your clone source and pastes the copies over the pixels that are currently underneath your tool cursor, as shown in the figure to the right.

If you drag instead of click, the clone source cursor moves in tandem with your tool cursor, and you clone a continuous strip of pixels along the length of your drag.

In the figure to the right, for example, the black crosshair shows the initial position of the clone source cursor. By dragging upward, I cloned the strip of pixels between the black crosshair cursor and the white crosshair cursor. The round cursor in the cloned strip represents my Clone tool cursor.

The Aligned option determines what happens on your *second* cloning click or drag. If you turn off the option, the clone source cursor returns to its original position, and you reclone the same pixels. As an example, I set the clone source in the spot indicated in the preceding figures. Then I dragged horizontally four times with the Aligned option turned off. The result is four duplicates of the same area.

If you turn on the Aligned option, however, the clone source cursor does not scurry back to its original position after your first cloning pass. Instead, it remains at its current location, and when you next click or drag, you continue cloning from where you left off. I dragged four times with the Aligned option turned on to create the second example.

In practical terms, then, you turn off the Aligned option if you want to clone the same pixels repeatedly and turn it on to avoid doing so. There's no "best" choice here — the right setting depends on the repair you need to make. (And trust me, all this becomes clearer when you actually work with the tool.)

No matter which option you pick, you can always Alt+click (Windows) or Option+click (Mac) to set a new clone source at any time.

Clone source   Cloned pixels

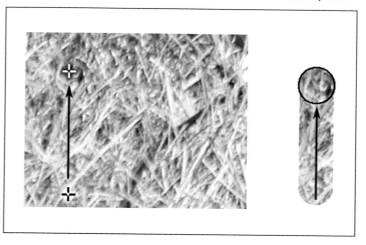

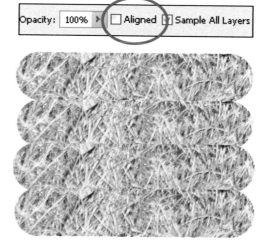

Clone Away Intrusive Objects *(continued)*

⑦ Turn on the Sample All Layers option.

This option enables the tool to clone pixels from your original image layer onto your new layer.

⑧ Click on or drag over the pixels you want to hide.

Again, if you click, you set down one brush-cursor's worth of cloned pixels. Drag to clone a continuous stroke of pixels.

Remember: On your second click or drag, the clone source cursor returns to its original position if you turned off the Aligned option. Otherwise, you keep cloning from the spot where you just left off. To reset the clone source, just Alt+click (Windows) or Option+click (Mac).

If you mess up, choose Edit⇨Undo to remove your last cloning stroke. You also can use the Eraser tool on your cloning layer to rub out mistakes.

Note: When cloning a large area, it's a good idea to clone from several sources. Otherwise, you can introduce a visible pattern in an area that should be random.

I cloned from several patches of grass, for example, to repair my image. In the tire area, I cloned pixels immediately above the cable so that the shadows and highlights of my clones would match their neighbors. You can see a close-up of my finished repair to the right.

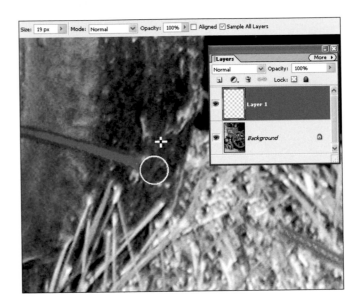

⑨ When you finish cloning, choose Layer⇨Flatten Image.

This step fuses your cloning layer to the original image.

Author Confidential

Save Your Work in the Right Format

After you finish retouching a photo, never save the file in the JPEG file format. Detailed fully in Chapter 1, this format applies lossy compression to the image, which eliminates some picture data in order to produce smaller files. Too much compression can destroy picture quality.

Instead, save edited pictures in a format that doesn't apply lossy compression — a *nondestructive* format,

in imaging lingo. If you use Photoshop Elements, the program's own format, PSD, is a good choice. (PSD is also the Photoshop format.) If you use some other program or if you need to open your picture in a program that doesn't recognize PSD, choose TIFF. Like PSD, TIFF is nondestructive, and you can open TIFF files in most print-publishing and word-processing programs.

Apply a Blur to Diminish Noise

Chapter 1 alerts you to the possible down-side to raising your camera's ISO setting: an increase in image *noise*. This defect, which gives your image a grainy look, can also occur with very long exposures or in pictures shot in dim lighting.

If you do wind up with a noisy image, you may be able to improve it by applying a blur filter in your photo editor. Some photo editors, including Photoshop Elements, even offer a specialized blur filter that's designed to tackle noise.

Even the most sophisticated blur filter, however, can't always distinguish noise from important image details. So you have to be careful about how you go about the noise-removal process. Here's the technique that I use:

① Select the areas where noise is most apparent.

In most cases, noise is most visible in areas that contain little detail or are softly focused, such as the background in the turtle image. Select just those areas, turning to the end of Chapter 1 if you need help. I selected just the background in my image; you can see my selection outline to the right.

② Choose Filter⇨Noise⇨ Reduce Noise.

You see the Reduce Noise dialog box. Select the Preview check box so that you can monitor the filter effects both in the image window and in the dialog box.

➌ If your image also suffers from JPEG artifacts, select the Remove JPEG Artifact check box.

When enabled, this option applies a blur that is designed to soften the blocky look that can occur with a high level of JPEG compression.

My turtle image doesn't have this problem, so I disabled the option. Note that JPEG artifacts are extremely difficult to remove successfully, so don't expect this feature to work any miracles. To avoid artifacting issues, follow the guidelines laid out in Chapter 1.

➍ Adjust the three sliders to find a balance between noise removal and detail preservation.

The Strength slider tackles *luminance noise,* which looks like monochromatic speckles. The Reduce Color Noise slider, curiously enough, goes after *color noise,* which looks a lot like luminance noise except that it features speckles of random colors. (You can see an illustration of both in Chapter 1; see the section related to Camera Raw files.)

As you raise either value, Elements applies blurring routines that are engineered to soften the specific type of noise. The higher you go, the stronger the blur is and the more image detail you lose.

The Preserve Details option enables you to limit the blurring effect to areas that don't contain detail. Raise the value to hold onto more detail — but understand that as you do, less noise will be removed.

There's no right combination of settings — you have to experiment to see which values work best for your image. I used the values shown in the dialog box at the top of the page for the turtle image.

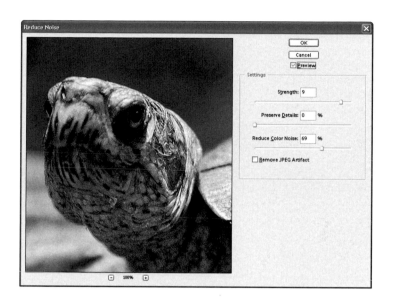

Apply a Blur to Diminish Noise *(continued)*

⑤ Click OK to close the dialog box.

If you're happy with the results, you're done. But if some areas of the image need additional work, move on to Step 6.

⑥ Choose Select➪Deselect.

This step gets rid of the selection outline you created in Step 1.

⑦ Use the Blur tool to clean up the rest of the image.

The Blur tool, which I introduce to you in Chapter 3, lives near the bottom of the toolbox. Set the tool Mode to Normal, the Strength to 30 percent, and turn on the Sample All Layers check box.

Working with a small, hard brush, rub the tool over areas that remain noisy, being careful to stay away from high-detail regions. Take a "stay within the lines" approach to this step. That is, avoid blurring any *edges* — boundaries along color or brightness transitions.

For example, I blurred the areas between the black stripes in the turtle's snout. You can see a close-up look at the results of all my noise-blurring in the After image to the right. The noise isn't entirely gone, but it's much less distracting than in the original image. In fact, unless you were to print the image very large, you probably wouldn't notice the noise at all.

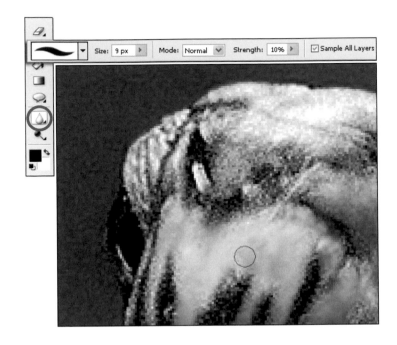

Before

After

After

Make a High-Resolution Image Web Friendly

Preparing a photo for the Web involves two steps:

➤ First, unless you shoot very low-resolution images, you must drastically reduce your pixel count. Otherwise, your image will be too large to view without scrolling, like the picture shown here.

➤ Second, you must save the file in the JPEG format, which is the only good image format that's recognized by all Web browsers and e-mail programs. Saving to this format also compresses the image, resulting in smaller files and shorter download times.

Photoshop Elements, like many programs, offers a one-step tool that enables you to trim pixels and preview your image at various JPEG compression settings. As I discuss in Chapter 1, increasing compression reduces file size but also lowers image quality. The previews help you find the best balance between quality and file size — which is why this kind of tool is referred to as a *JPEG optimizer.*

To use the Elements version of this tool, follow these steps:

❶ Choose File⇨Save for Web.

You see the Save For Web dialog box. Inside the dialog box, the left preview shows you the image at its current state. The right preview displays the image as it will appear if saved at the current dialog box settings.

To zoom in on the image, click the Zoom tool icon in the upper-left corner of the dialog box. Then click either preview. To zoom out, press Alt (Windows) or Option (Mac) as you click. To scroll the display, drag inside the preview with the Hand tool.

Make a High-Resolution Image Web Friendly *(continued)*

➋ Set the preferred modem speed.

The current image file size appears below each preview. For the After preview, the program also estimates the time required to download the image over an Internet connection running at the speed shown.

You can specify the connection speed for this preview via the pop-up menu shown in the figure to the right. To open the menu, click the little arrow circled in the figure. Unless you're sharing the image *only* with people who have a high-speed connection, I suggest setting the connection speed at 56.6 Kbps (kilobytes per second), the current norm for dial-up connections.

➌ Check the Image Size values to see whether you need to dump pixels.

How many pixels do you need? Here's a little background to help you make the call: A computer monitor, like your camera, produces images by using pixels. How many monitor pixels are available depends on the screen settings you use. Most computers allow you to choose from a variety of settings — 800 x 600 pixels, 1024 x 768, 1600 x 1200, and so on.

When you display a digital photo, one screen pixel is assigned to every image pixel. So you have to set the image pixel count according to how much screen real estate you want the picture to consume.

For example, the portrait featured here is 800 pixels wide by 600 pixels tall. On a monitor set to the 800 x 600 display setting, the image fills the entire screen, as shown in the illustration to the right — again, there's a

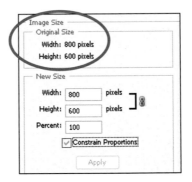

600 pixels

800 pixels

1-to-1 relationship between screen and image pixels. If you change the display setting to 1600 x 1200, the same image fills one-quarter of the monitor, as shown in the second figure.

Remember, though, that the e-mail window eats up part of the screen. So when attaching pictures to e-mail messages, I generally limit the pixel count to 400 pixels horizontally and 350 vertically. If you're preparing an image for a Web page, you may want a larger or smaller image depending on the design.

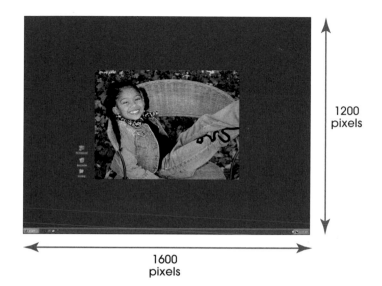

1200 pixels

1600 pixels

❹ Enter new pixel dimensions if necessary.

First, select the Constrain Proportions check box so that you retain the original proportions of your image when you resize it. Then enter the desired width, in pixels, in the Width box. Or enter the desired height in the Height box. When you change one value, the other changes automatically.

Note: Be sure to click the Apply button after you enter the new values. The file size on the After preview should drop when this step is completed.

❺ Select JPEG High from the Preset drop-down list at the top of the dialog box.

This option specifies JPEG as your file format and selects a minimum level of compression, which results in a high level of image quality. Remember: The setting names reflect the resulting image quality, *not* the amount of compression.

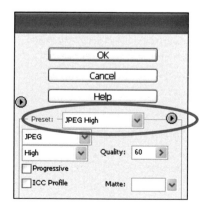

Make a High-Resolution Image Web Friendly *(continued)*

⑥ Use the Quality slider to fine-tune the compression amount.

Experiment to find a good balance between quality and file size. (As soon as you drag the slider, the Preset option changes to Custom.)

Again, a higher Quality value results in *less* compression, which means better images but larger file sizes. As you play with the slider, the preview window updates to show you the image quality you can expect, and the file size and download estimate values also change to reflect the compression setting.

Generally speaking, keep your picture file sizes below 100K if you want to stay in good standing with people on your e-mail list. For a Web page, you probably need to go even lower, especially if you have multiple images on the page.

⑦ Deselect the Progressive and ICC Profile check boxes.

Both options can cause display problems with some Web browsers and e-mail programs. The ICC Profile option, which enables you to embed a color profile in the file, also increases file size.

Ignore the Matte option altogether; it's relevant only if the background layer of your image contains transparent pixels. And unless you've done some specialized layers work in your photo editor, your background layer won't qualify.

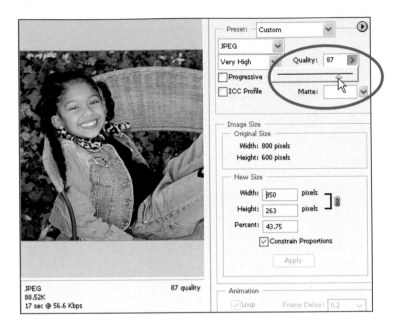

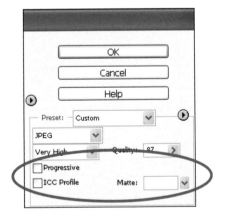

⑧ Click OK.

You now see the Save Optimized As dialog box, which looks and works almost exactly like the standard Save As dialog box. Give your image a name and click Save. Be sure to use a different name than your original image; you may want the original file with all its pixels intact some day.

After you click save, the dialog box closes, and Elements stores the Web copy in the location you specified in the Save Optimized As dialog box. Your original image remains on-screen.

When you close the original image, you're asked again whether you want to save any changes you made to the photo. It's okay to do so — the changes you made via the Save for Web dialog box affect only the Web copy.

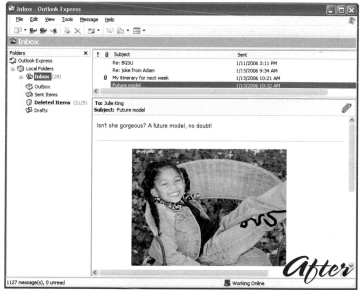

6 EXTREME MAKEOVERS

When you're first starting to expand your photography knowledge, remembering how to address one creative or technical problem is difficult enough. Getting a grip on how to manipulate several different aspects of a picture is even more daunting.

Which brings me to the title of this chapter: These last makeovers *are* extreme in that you can see a dramatic difference between the Before and After images. But the solutions used to transform the images are far from extraordinary. In fact, most of the camera controls and shooting strategies you can read about in this chapter have been explained individually in earlier chapters.

These makeovers, however, combine several troubleshooting techniques. My hope is that as you review these last examples, you'll gain a better understanding of how to put all your newfound photography skills together to perform your own extreme makeovers.

Turn Sorry Snapshots into Framable Winners

In my experience, the most meaningful portraits aren't the formal, posed kind taken in a professional studio. Rather, they're snapshots that capture spontaneous moments of joy and interaction between friends and family.

"Spontaneous snapshot," however, doesn't mean that you can't spend a few seconds considering the best way to record such moments. If you don't, your results can easily look like the Before picture here: a potentially super shot ruined by too many photographic flaws. In this case, the subjects are underexposed due to strong backlighting, and sunlight reflecting off the lens caused lens flare. That's not to mention the composition: The background is ugly, and there's too much of it — the subjects almost get lost in the frame.

Here's a step-by-step look at how to solve these problems and take this kind of picture from Before to After:

❶ To brighten backlit subjects, increase the exposure.

When you shoot in autoexposure mode, a very bright background can fool the camera into thinking that it should produce a darker exposure than what you need. Your camera's EV compensation setting enables you to capture a brighter or darker exposure than the camera originally selects. This option is available in program autoexposure (AE) mode, aperture-priority AE mode, or shutter-priority AE mode and is usually labeled with a little plus/minus sign like the one highlighted to the right.

A higher EV number produces a brighter picture; a lower value, a darker exposure. I raised the EV setting to +1.0 to produce this second shot. Before snapping the picture, I scanned the frame for lens flare and then eliminated it by using my hand as an awning.

Alternate Method: If your camera also offers a choice of autoexposure metering modes, changing from pattern metering — or whatever mode on your camera bases exposure on the entire frame — to center- or spot-weighted metering can help in backlit situations as well. For my money, though, it's usually easier to simply use the EV control.

Of course, if your camera offers manual-exposure control, you can simply open the aperture or slow the shutter speed as needed to brighten the exposure.

Chapter 2 provides complete details about EV compensation, metering modes, lens flare, and other exposure-related issues.

❷ If possible, reposition the subjects to avoid backlighting and provide a simple backdrop.

Although raising the EV setting to +1.0 exposed the faces of my subjects properly, their hair is now greatly overexposed. And there's still that distracting background to address.

To eliminate the backlighting problem and provide a nicer backdrop in one step, I repositioned my subjects in front of a stand of evergreens. Then I changed the EV setting back to a neutral 0.0 and retook the shot. You see the much improved result to the right.

EV +1.0

EV 0.0, 46mm, f/7.1

Turn Sorry Snapshots into Framable Winners *(continued)*

❸ Shorten depth of field to soften the background and emphasize your subjects.

The pine trees provide a much nicer backdrop, but the many angles and curves of the branches still attract the eye a little too much. The solution is to use camera settings that shorten depth of field or the zone of sharp focus. As explored in Chapter 3, you can shorten depth of field in three ways:

➤ Move closer to your subject.

➤ Zoom in.

➤ Enlarge the aperture (choose a lower f-stop number).

I opted for the second and third solutions. I zoomed from an original focal length of 42mm, shown with Step 2, to 70mm, and I opened the aperture from f/7.1 to f/4.5. This both softened the background and reduced the amount of background, as shown in the image to the right.

To specify the aperture setting on a camera that does not offer manual-exposure control, switch to aperture-priority auto-exposure, if available. This mode is typically represented on a camera dial by the letter *A* or *Av*. What if your camera has no aperture-priority mode? Look for a Portrait setting, typically represented by a symbol that looks like a head or torso, as shown to the right. This mode usually results in the largest aperture setting your camera allows.

EV 0.0, 70mm, f/4.5

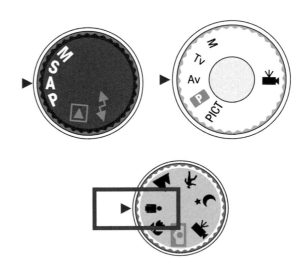

Remember: Although the amount of background that remains in my example may still seem a little much, I framed the shot this loosely so that I would be able to crop it to fit any traditional frame size — 4 x 6 inches, 5 x 7, or 8 x 10. If you don't leave a little extra margin in your digital photos, you may have to clip off part of your subject to fit those frame sizes. See Chapter 1 for an illustration.

❹ For outdoor portraits, use fill flash to bring the eyes out of the shadows.

At this point, I'm happy with the backdrop, but the subjects' faces are just slightly underexposed. Adding flash can almost always improve outdoor portraits, as it did here. The flash throws some additional light on the faces, bringing eyes out of the shadows. And, depending on the time of day and brightness of the sun, using a flash can also create a slight warming effect, adding a nice golden tone to the skin.

To use flash outdoors, however, you must select the force flash or fill flash setting (the name varies depending on the camera). In automatic-flash mode, the light must be very dim for the camera to fire the flash. Fill (or force) flash is usually indicated by a single lightning-bolt symbol like the one in the top image.

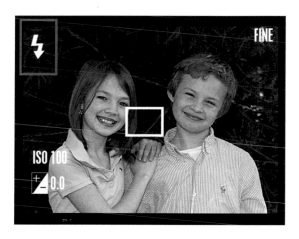

EV 0.0, 70mm, f/4.5, with flash

Turn Sorry Snapshots into Framable Winners *(continued)*

⑤ To warm skin tones further, set the white-balance option to Cloudy.

This setting may be called Shade or Overcast, depending on the camera, but it's usually represented by a little cloud icon like the one shown to the right. How much your colors change depends on the actual lighting conditions. For the full story on white balance, see Chapter 4.

Alternate Method: You can also warm skin tones by using a warming filter or a gold reflector. Chapter 4 offers a look at a warming filter and shows you how to add this color effect in your photo editor. Chapter 2 gives you a look at a reflector.

Author Confidential

Retail Printing: Faster, Cheaper, Easier

Until recently, digital photo printing was a do-it-yourself proposition. And the job quickly became tiresome if you had more than a few images to print. Fortunately, getting prints made is now fast and easy, thanks to the introduction of new retail printing options.

Online services such as Kodak Gallery, Snapfish, and Shutterfly provide both printing and photo-sharing services, for example. You just upload your picture files and specify where you want the pictures delivered.

For local service, just about any place that used to process film can make digital prints. And many labs are linked to online networks that offer the ultimate in convenience: You upload your pictures, choose a local lab to do the printing, and then pick up your prints a few hours later. (To find these services in your area, start at www.digitalcameradeveloping.com or www.prints-are-memories.com.)

Prices range from about 12 cents to 24 cents for a 4 x 6 print — typically, less than the cost of the ink and paper needed for home photo printing.

My final portrait appears below. Although I needed a few pages to spell out all the steps, snapping better portraits really boils down to a few key points:

➤ Choose a complementary background.

➤ If subjects are backlit and underexposed and you're shooting in an autoexposure mode, raise the EV compensation setting or try a different metering mode.

➤ Zoom in and open the aperture to create a nicer background. (Work in Portrait mode if you can't select a specific aperture.)

➤ When shooting outdoors, use fill flash to brighten faces. For indoor portrait lighting tips, see Chapter 2.

➤ Set the camera to Cloudy whitebalance mode to warm skin tones (works only if actual light isn't cloudy).

Take a Low-Light Landscape from Dark and Drab to Bright and Fab

A word of advice about photographing the ruins at Pompeii: You need more than a few hours of daylight to do the site justice. I speak from experience: A recent trip took me to that fascinating spot but provided only a 4-hour window in which to shoot. I arrived mid-afternoon and spent the next three hours racing through the maze of ruins and walkways trying to get all the shots that caught my eye — which, as you can imagine, were endless.

When the daylight began to fade, I could see right away that the sunset was going to be spectacular, and I wanted to find just the right vantage point from which to shoot it through an interesting arch or window. Unfortunately, by the time I finally found a good spot, the sun had receded enough that I faced a no-win exposure challenge: If I chose settings that properly exposed the sky, which was still fairly bright, the foreground became too dark, as shown in the top image to the right. If I based the exposure on the fore-ground, on the other hand, the sky was over-exposed, with all the beautiful pale highlights blown out to white, as in the lower image.

Well, because I wasn't going to have the opportunity to come back for another sun-set shoot, I decided on the first option. I exposed the images for the sky tones I wanted and just hoped that I would be able to rescue at least some shadow detail in my photo editor. In most cases, this is the way to go. A good photo-editing program usually can unearth more shadow detail than the human eye can detect, but the same isn't true for highlights.

In fact, turning out a pretty good image proved easier than I expected. These steps show you how to perform similar miracles in your exposure-challenged images. (The steps feature Photoshop Elements, but you can find similar tools in most good photo-editing programs.)

❶ Choose Enhance⇨ Adjust Lighting⇨Shadows/Highlights.

This command calls up the Shadows/ Highlights filter, which is a great tool for rescuing hidden image detail from the shadows.

After choosing the command, you see the Shadows/Highlights dialog box, shown to the right. By default, the Lighten Shadows control is set to 25%, producing an immediate brightening of the image. (Be sure to select the Preview check box so that your adjustments are visible in the image window.)

❷ Drag the Lighten Shadows slider to the right as needed.

You can also tone down highlights by using the Darken Highlights slider and adjust contrast of the midtones by using the Midtone Contrast slider.

For this image, I set the Lighten Shadows control to 50. The result is pretty dramatic. But the highlights actually need a little brightening, not darkening, so I left the Darken Highlights slider set to 0. You see the result to the right.

If you're happy with your image at this point, just click OK to close the filter dialog box and move on. But in many cases, you may need to follow up the Shadows/Highlights

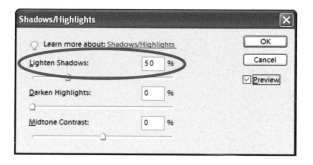

Take a Low-Light Landscape from Dark and Drab to Bright and Fab *(continued)*

filter with the Levels filter and/or the Hue/ Saturation filter. The example image could benefit from both filters.

❸ Apply the Levels filter if needed.

Explained fully in Chapter 2, the Levels filter performs the opposite function of Shadows/ Highlights. With Levels, you can make shadows darker and highlights brighter.

Choose Enhance➪Adjust Lighting➪ Levels to display the Levels dialog box, shown to the right. You manipulate midtones, highlights, and shadows by dragging the sliders underneath the histogram. The left slider controls shadows; the middle slider, midtones; and the right slider, highlights.

I wanted to make the brightest sky pixels just a tad brighter, so I dragged the Highlights slider to the position shown in the dialog box. Then I dragged the Midtones slider slightly left to brighten the midtones a little as well.

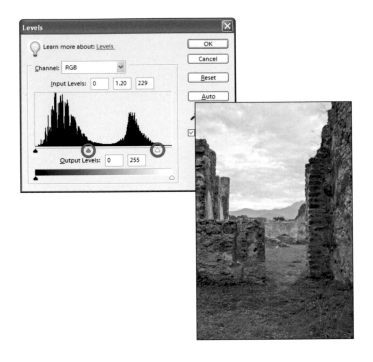

❹ Increase color saturation if desired.

Applying the Levels filter often has a side effect of sucking some color out of a photo. In this case, it's hard to tell whether saturation was lost or just never there originally, but it's clear that strengthening saturation would improve the image.

To boost saturation in Elements, choose Enhance➪Adjust Color➪Adjust Hue/Saturation. You see the dialog box shown to the right. Drag the Saturation slider to the right to increase saturation. I set the Saturation value to +20 to produce the image accompanying the dialog box.

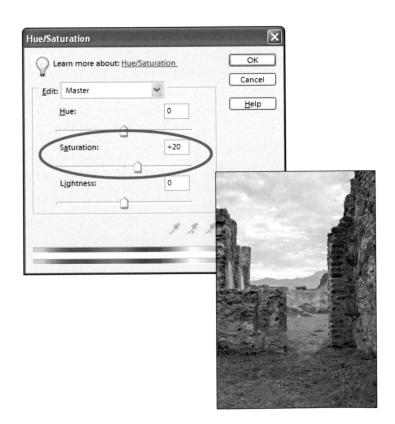

⑤ Add a virtual warming filter to emphasize the sunset glow.

Photographers refer to the hour just before sunset as the "golden hour" because the light has a beautiful golden tone. But after all the manipulation to exposure and color that I applied to my Pompeii image, whatever glow might have been present was lost.

Adding some warmth back to the scene is a snap with the Elements Photo Filter, first introduced in Chapter 4. Choose Filter⇨ Adjustments⇨Photo Filter to display the filter dialog box. I selected the Warming Filter (85) option from the filter list and cranked the Density slider up to 30 to produce my final image.

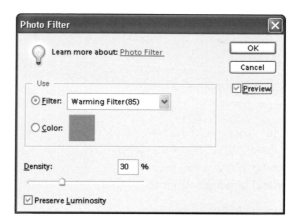

Turn a Blurry Mess into an Animal Adventure

One day, I hope to have enough money and time to go on a real African safari — the kind where you shoot with a camera, not guns. Until then, the local zoo provides my only opportunities to photograph wildlife other than my dog and the squirrels that drive him batty.

Zoo photography presents several challenges, unfortunately. First, the cages and fences that keep the animals safe from humans tend to throw autofocus systems for a loop. Instead of locking focus on the animal, the camera hones in on the fence, and you get a result like the Before picture here. Second, zoo-goers are kept at a substantial distance from most animals, which means that even with a powerful zoom lens, you're hard-pressed to get a good close-up or even compose an image that doesn't contain an excess of background.

You can take a few steps to get the best possible zoo pictures, however. Part of the magic happens before you take the shot; the rest involves some simple digital-darkroom tricks.

❶ Use the highest picture-quality settings on your camera.

Capture the image at your camera's highest resolution and choose Raw, TIFF, or the best-quality JPEG setting as the file format. Using these high-quality settings enables you to crop the picture and enlarge the remainder without seeing a big drop-off in picture quality. Remember, the impact of too few pixels and too much compression becomes more apparent as you enlarge the image.

Turn off digital zoom also. Digital zoom is nothing more than in-camera cropping and enlarging, and it leads to lower-quality images.

For the full story on resolution, format, digital zoom, and other picture-quality issues, see Chapter 1.

❷ Set the shutter speed high enough to accommodate any unexpected movement.

Unless you're trying to shoot a flying bird or running animal, a shutter speed of 1/250 or higher should be fine. To specify shutter speed, you must switch to manual-exposure mode or shutter-priority mode, usually indicated by the letters *S* or *Tv*. If your camera doesn't offer either mode, try Action mode, if available. This mode results in a faster shutter speed. (See Chapter 3 for more tips on shooting action.)

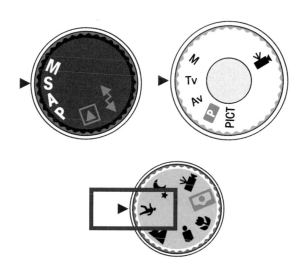

Author Confidential

How to Photograph Through Glass

A few tricks will help you to photograph zoo inhabitants that are kept behind glass. First, turn off your flash; it usually creates a reflection in the glass. No flash means that you probably need a slow shutter to properly expose the image, however, so steady the camera to avoid the blur caused by camera shake. Finally, with an autofocus camera, be sure that the camera doesn't lock focus on the glass instead of the animal. If it does, place your lens right up against the glass rather than standing a few feet from it. If that isn't possible, lock focus on something outside the glass that's the same distance away. (See Step 3 of my baboon makeover to find out how.) Remember, however, that in autoexposure mode, exposure and focus are set together, so lock focus on something that's similar in brightness to your subject.

Turn a Blurry Mess into an Animal Adventure (continued)

Julie's Take: If you want as much of the scene in focus as possible, also stop down the aperture — that is, choose a higher f-stop number — to extend depth of field. How far you can go depends on the lighting conditions, of course. In very bright light, you should be able to combine a fast shutter and small aperture; on overcast days, you're more restricted.

If you're working in shutter-priority mode, reducing the shutter speed causes the camera to stop down the aperture. In Action mode, unfortunately, you can't specify a certain shutter speed. So if depth of field is more important than shutter speed and the animals you're photographing are slow movers, you may want to work in Landscape mode instead. This mode uses settings that produce the greatest depth of field. The Chapter 3 makeover featuring the rhinoceroses — rhinoceri? — offers an illustration of how switching to Landscape mode can affect your picture.

❸ Give the autofocus system a hand.

If the camera's autofocus mechanism has trouble finding the right focus point through a fence or cage bars, first determine the camera's current autofocus zone: Is it the closest object, the center of the frame, or some other area? (Chapter 3 explains these issues.) Switch to center-area focusing, if you have a choice; other zones may make it impossible for the camera to focus on anything other than the fence.

Most cameras indicate the autofocus zone with a small rectangle. Frame the image so that the animal is within that zone, as illustrated to the right, and lock in focus by pressing and holding the shutter button

halfway. Then you can reframe the picture as you see fit and press the shutter the rest of the way. I used this trick to bring the baboons into focus and capture the image to the right. The foreground fence almost seems to disappear, although you can still make out some of it in certain areas such as the tail and haunches of the larger baboon.

If you don't have any luck using this technique, try locking focus on an object that's outside the fence but the same distance from your lens as the animal.

Again, remember that in autoexposure mode, exposure is set when you lock in focus. So make sure that the placeholder object on which you lock focus isn't substantially darker or brighter than your subject.

❹ Crop the image to eliminate excess background.

In Elements, select the Crop tool, highlighted to the right. Set the tool options as shown in the figure and drag to create a crop outline around the area you want to keep.

When you release the mouse button, you can adjust the outline by dragging the boxes around its perimeter. To reposition the outline, drag inside it. Finally, click the green Accept checkmark at the bottom of the crop outline to apply the crop. I cropped my picture to include just the larger baboon, as shown to the right.

Alternate Method: If you need your cropped image to be a specific size, follow the instructions in Chapter 5 for using the Crop command instead of the Crop tool. With the command, you can specify exact dimensions for your crop outline.

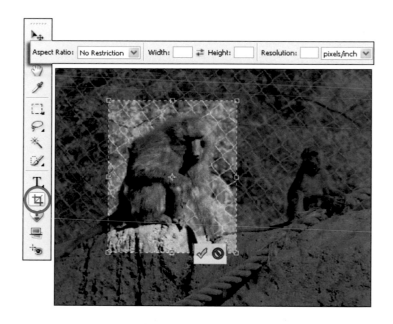

Turn a Blurry Mess into an Animal Adventure *(continued)*

⑤ Clone away any remaining fence.

The Clone tool, detailed in Chapter 5, enables you to copy "good" pixels over "bad" ones. I cloned surrounding pixels over the few segments of the fence that remained visible in the baboon. Then I went a step further and also removed the background fence, setting my primate friend free to roam the streets of Indianapolis. You can see a bit of that process as well as the final result in the figures to the right.

Julie's Take: Be judicious in making this kind of serious alteration to a photograph. If you're producing a picture for your own enjoyment, "reinventing reality" is fine. But don't try to sell or represent your altered image as something it isn't. I wouldn't try to market this picture to a company producing a brochure for a real safari, for example. And if you're retouching a product photo, you enter the danger zone when you try to make the item appear better than it is in real life.

Anyway, the cloned photo looks pretty good at first glance, but has two problems upon closer inspection. First, all the cloning I did to the background left it looking a little odd — in some areas, you can make out distinct leaf and branch edges, but in other areas, the foliage blurs together. Second, the baboon is a little soft in the focus department.

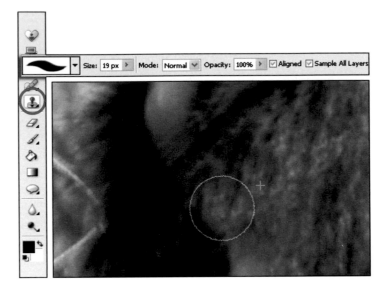

⑥ Selectively adjust focus if needed.

To make the repaired background a little more believable, I used the blur technique outlined in Chapter 3. Using the Elements Selection Brush, I first masked the baboon and then applied the Gaussian Blur filter to just the background. This step had two benefits: It hid the textural discrepancies created by my cloning and also drew more attention to the baboon, now sharper than the background in comparison.

Next, I selected the baboon and deselected the background. Then I applied the Unsharp Mask filter, also covered in Chapter 3, to sharpen the animal only.

Note: When creating my initial mask with the Selection Brush, I used a soft-edged brush around the boundary between baboon and background. A soft brush results in a feathered selection outline, which causes any subsequent filter you apply to fade in gradually along the boundaries of the outline. This technique is helpful when you're trying to select an animal with fur (or a person with hair). Selecting each strand of fur or hair is nearly impossible, but by feathering the selection outline, you can make sure there's no obvious break between your sharpened and unsharpened areas.

You see the end result of my selective blurring and sharpening to the right.

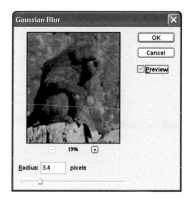

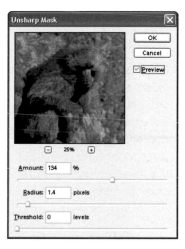

Turn a Blurry Mess into an Animal Adventure *(continued)*

⑦ Adjust exposure and saturation selectively to further draw attention to the subject.

Applying a slight increase in contrast to just your subject can further separate it from the background. To increase contrast, use the Levels filter, explained in Chapter 2. In Elements, choose Enhance⇨Adjust Lighting⇨Levels to open the filter dialog box. Drag the Shadows slider to the right to make shadows darker; drag the Highlights slider to the left, as shown in the dialog box to the right, to make highlights brighter. Adjust the Midtones slider as needed after setting your new shadow and highlight points. I applied the Levels settings shown in the figure.

You can also increase saturation of your subject and decrease saturation of the background to draw more attention to the subject. In Elements, choose Enhance⇨Adjust Colors⇨Adjust Hue/Saturation to open the Hue/Saturation filter dialog box.

For this image, I set the Saturation slider to +17, as shown in the figure, to boost saturation of the baboon slightly. Then I applied the opposite change to the background, setting the slider to –17 to suck some color out of the leaves. (See Chapter 4 for additional information about saturation and this filter.)

The final result of all this monkey business (oh, I crack myself up) appears to the right.

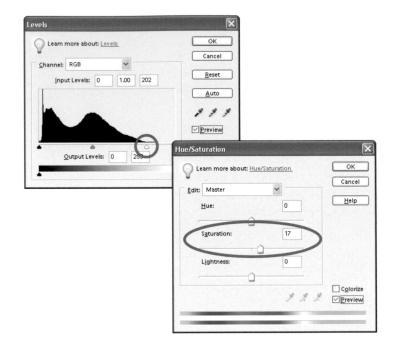

Give Your Product Shots More Sales Appeal

Suppose that you were searching online shopping sites looking for a vintage coffee set to give to a pair of antiques lovers as a wedding present. If you saw a picture like the one to the right, would you be inclined to buy, even if the product itself were just what you wanted? The set is poorly displayed, the background is ugly, the lighting is bad, and the picture quality is blotchy, with lots of color distortion. Overall, this image leaves the impression that the seller isn't a serious merchant.

Now suppose that you found the exact same coffee set on another site, for the same price, but the product photo looked like the After picture shown a few pages from here. My guess is that you'd be more comfortable buying from the second seller.

Julie's Take: You're probably thinking that I went to great lengths to make the Before picture look as horrible as possible, and it's true. But I did so because I see so many similar images during my online shopping sprees.

You *don't* have to go to great lengths to produce a more appealing product shot, however. Just a few simple changes can make an incredible difference in how your products — and your business — are perceived.

The following steps explain how to overhaul your product shots:

Give Your Product Shots More Sales Appeal *(continued)*

❶ Stage the product against a simple but complementary backdrop.

Spend just a few minutes thinking about the best display arrangement — one that shows the product detail the buyer needs but also is attractive from a compositional standpoint. For example, I spread out the china pieces as shown to the right. The arrangement of the pieces provides some visual interest and also lets the buyer see each individual plate, which is important for someone buying a set of items.

I also draped a piece of subtly patterned blue fabric behind the coffee set. You don't have to spend money for professional photography backdrops; just visit your local fabric store and head for the remnants table. I think I paid a whopping $2 for this blue piece, for example. I've even been known to drag out a skirt or dress that has a nice pattern to use as a background.

❷ Shoot at the highest-quality JPEG setting.

Although the restaged photo is much improved, it still has a huge problem: So much JPEG compression was applied that the colors are distorted and the image appears blotchy.

Detailed in Chapter 1, JPEG compression is a process that occurs when you capture an image in the JPEG file format. To avoid the kind of JPEG defects you see in the shot to the right, select the JPEG option that applies the *least* compression — in other words, the highest-quality JPEG option.

Also avoid editing and resaving your photo in the JPEG format multiple times, because each time you save, you make the problem worse. When you do save your photo in this format, always choose the highest-quality JPEG setting, as you do on your camera.

To produce the better-quality product shot to the right, I captured the image at my camera's highest JPEG setting, opened the image once to crop it and size it for the Web, and then saved it as a JPEG file, again using the highest-quality option. You can see a huge difference in the image quality, especially in the close-up shot.

For even better results, you can shoot in the TIFF or Camera Raw format, also explained in Chapter 1, if your camera offers those choices. Then create a JPEG copy for your online use. That way, your image undergoes just one round of compression.

Remember: If you plan to use your product shot in printed material, be sure to also follow the resolution guidelines laid out in Chapter 1 to ensure good print quality. For online use, see the instructions in Chapter 5 about sizing and saving a Web-friendly image.

❸ Pay attention to lighting; shoot flash-free if possible.

Although the quality and staging of my product shot now are on target, the lighting leaves a lot to be desired. I shot the image with my camera's onboard flash, resulting in harsh shadows behind the pitcher and two standing plates as well as under the flat plates. In addition, the light from the flash is reflected in the china in several spots, creating flares that wash out details.

The Chapter 2 makeovers featuring the train and jewelry photos offer specific tips

Give Your Product Shots More Sales Appeal *(continued)*

for improving your product lighting, so I won't go into all of them here. To solve the lighting problems in my china image, I shot the product inside a light tent. This diffused the light, creating softer shadows and eliminating the flash reflections. Instead of using flash, I lit the product with two lamps, placing one on either side of the light tent. (You can see a picture of a light tent in the Chapter 2 makeover.) The resulting shot appears to the right.

Julie's Take: To be honest, even a light tent sometimes doesn't enable you to eliminate *all* reflections from glass, china, and other reflective surfaces. So just do the best you can and then use your photo editor's Clone tool to patch over any remaining reflections or flares.

❹ Stop down the aperture as much as possible to keep more of the frame in sharp focus.

I'm assuming here that you want the entire shot to be in focus, of course, as would be the case for the china shot. The top image on this page, for example, has a very shallow depth of field. As a result, focus on the coffee pot and two upright plates is sharp, but the foreground plates are blurry. Because a prospective buyer would want a clear view of the entire set, the depth of field should be extended.

As covered in Chapter 3, one way to increase depth of field is to stop down the aperture (choose a higher f-stop number). I shifted from f/4.5 to f/16 to produce the image to the right. Now all the china is in focus.

f/4.5, 70mm

f/16, 70mm

Remember: Stopping down the aperture means that you need to decrease shutter speed to produce the same exposure. If the shutter speed falls below 1 / 60 second or so, get a tripod to ensure that no camera shake blurs your shot. Chapter 3 offers some additional tips on keeping the camera steady.

❺ To bring even more of the image into focus, zoom out and move away as far as possible.

Zooming out also increases depth of field. So if your camera has a zoom lens — a true optical zoom, not a digital zoom — zoom out to the camera's widest angle.

Still need more depth of field? Move farther from your product. The greater your subject-to-lens distance, the greater the depth of field. Don't worry about framing the image correctly — you can crop away the excess background in your photo editor.

To produce the top image to the right, I kept the aperture at f / 16, zoomed out from a focal length of 70mm to 42mm, and moved as far back from the product as my room space allowed. (Chapter 3 explains focal length.)

❻ Crop the image as needed.

Chapter 5 explains two different ways to crop a photo. I used the Crop tool to produce the final image to the right. Keep in mind that online images benefit from tight cropping; every pixel you trim away decreases file size, which shortens download times.

f/16, 42mm

Appendix

GLOSSARY AND QUICK REFERENCE GUIDE

When I travel to a foreign country, I make it a point to learn a few key phrases in the native tongue: *please, thank you, hello, goodbye,* and, most essential, *where is the bathroom?* The trouble is that I'm not good with languages, so I often get the words mixed up. On a trip to China, for example, I was mortified when our guide gently informed me that the word I used repeatedly to thank our waiters during our meal actually meant "Goodbye!"

Learning the language of digital photography can seem just as confusing. Sorting out the camera lingo — aperture, f/stop, focal length, and the like — is challenging enough. If you add in all the terminology associated with the digital darkroom, you have a vocabulary list that simply seems overwhelming.

Throughout the book, you can find detailed explanations of all the important digital photography terms you need to know to take full advantage of your camera. But when you need a little refresher or stumble across an unknown word as you explore a particular makeover, this appendix contains an extensive glossary of terms.

To help you remember how to put your understanding of aperture, focal length, and the like to practical use, the appendix also contains a few quick-reference charts, including one in which you can write down how you access various controls on your camera.

To wrap up the book, I provide a quick guide to implementing the color-management features found in Photoshop Elements 4.0. Before you dive into this section, first read the Chapter 1 section related to color spaces to get a general background that will help you better understand the color-management features.

Glossary of Digital Photography Terms

A

Adobe RGB: A generic color model, developed by Adobe Systems, that defines a wider gamut of colors than is included in the standard model used by digital cameras, sRGB. *See also* color model, sRGB. *(See Chapter 1 illustration.)*

aliasing: A defect that causes curved and diagonal lines to appear jagged. This defect is usually related to an inadequate number of image pixels. *(See Chapter 1 illustration.)*

anti-aliasing: An option available for some photo-editing tools; smoothes the jagged edges along curved and diagonal lines created by those tools.

aperture: One of three main components of a camera's light-gathering system; an opening in an adjustable diaphragm that permits light to strike the image sensor when the shutter is open. *(See Chapter 2 illustration.)*

aperture-priority autoexposure: A semi-automatic exposure mode found on some cameras. In this mode, you select the aperture (f-stop), and the camera automatically chooses the necessary shutter speed to properly expose the image. Useful for situations in which you want to control depth of field. Usually indicated on a camera dial by the letters *A* or *Av* (for *aperture value*).

artifact: Used to describe random color defects caused by too much JPEG compression. Can also occur as the result of an image-capture or file-processing problem. *(See Chapter 1 illustration.)*

aspect ratio: The ratio of image width to height, with width typically stated first. A roll of 35mm film has an aspect ratio of 3:2. The standard digital-camera image aspect ratio is 4:3, although some cameras offer a setting that creates a 3:2 image, as well.

autoexposure (AE): An exposure mode in which the camera measures the light in a scene and then selects the aperture and shutter speed required to capture the image at the current ISO. *See also* aperture-priority autoexposure, shutter-priority autoexposure.

autofocus zone: The area of the frame on which the camera's autofocus system establishes focus.

average metering: *See* pattern metering.

B

banding: A defect that creates abrupt breaks in what should be a smooth color transition; also known as *posterization*. Can occur when extreme exposure or color changes are applied in a photo editor. *(See Chapter 1 illustration.)*

bit: A basic unit of computer data.

bit depth: Refers to how many bits an image contains, which in turn determines how many colors are possible. More bits (a higher bit depth) mean a broader range of available colors. Most digital cameras capture 24-bit images, but higher-end models permit 48-bit images. Bit depth can also be defined as the number of bits per color channel; for example, a 24-bit RGB image has 8 bits per each of the three color channels.

bracketing: Taking several shots of the same scene at different exposure settings.

byte: A unit of computer data, equivalent to 8 bits.

C

Camera Raw: One of three digital-camera file formats currently in use. Usually available only on higher-end models. Records raw, "uncooked" data right from the image sensor without any of the picture processing that occurs when other formats are used. The photographer then opens the file in a conversion program and specifies how the raw data should be translated into a picture.

CCD: The most common type of imaging sensor used in digital cameras; stands for *charge-coupled device*.

CcMmYK: Some photo-quality printers have a six-color ink system for better color accuracy. The two additional colors usually are light cyan and light magenta, and this is often expressed as the CcMmYK color model. *See also* CMYK.

center-area autofocus: An autofocus mode in which the camera sets focus based on the object at the center of the frame.

center-weighted metering: An autoexposure mode in which the camera bases the exposure on the entire frame but gives more weight to the area at the center.

clipped highlights, clipped shadows: A loss of shadow or highlight detail that occurs as a result of an exposure adjustment, incorrect exposure settings, or poor camera performance. When highlights are clipped, very light areas become absolute white; when shadows are clipped, very dark pixels shift to absolute black.

Clone tool: Found in most photo-editing programs, a tool that enables you to duplicate pixels from one part of the image and paste them onto another area. Used to hide image flaws. *(See Chapter 5 illustration.)* May also be called *Clone Stamp* or *Rubber Stamp.*

closest-object autofocus: An autofocus mode in which the camera bases focus on the object nearest the lens.

CMOS: Along with CCD, one of two types of digital-camera image sensors. Stands for *complementary metal-oxide semiconductor* and is pronounced *see-moss.*

CMYK: A color model used to describe printers that mix *cyan, magenta, yellow,* and *black* inks to render images.

color channel: A virtual storage vat for specific brightness information in a digital image file. RGB images contain three channels, one each for the red, green, and blue brightness values.

colorimeter: A device that measures the display output of a computer monitor. Used to build color profiles as part of a color-management system.

color-management system (CMS): A combination of hardware and software tools used by some digital photographers to produce greater color consistency as an image moves from camera (or scanner) to monitor to printer. Serves as a sort of universal color translator, telling one device the best way to interpret the color values in an image file created by another device.

color model: A way of defining the primary colors that an imaging device (camera, scanner, printer, or monitor) uses to produce all other colors. Also refers to the spectrum of colors the device can generate.

Digital cameras, scanners, and monitors adhere to the RGB color model, mixing red, green, and blue light to produce color.

color profile: A data file that describes the color capabilities of an imaging device.

color space: *See* color model.

color temperature: Refers to the color cast emitted by a particular light source; measured on the Kelvin scale. *(See Chapter 4 illustration.)*

CompactFlash: A common type of digital-camera memory card.

compression: A process that occurs when you save an image file in some formats. Compression eliminates some image data in order to reduce the size of the file. *See also* lossless compression, lossy compression.

continuous autofocus: Offered by some cameras, a mode in which the camera continuously adjusts focus as you move the lens.

convergence: A phenomenon that causes vertical structures to appear to lean either to the center or outer edges of a photograph. Usually occurs when shooting with a wide-angle lens (which has a short focal length).

creative scene modes: *See* scene modes.

D

depth of field (DOF): Describes the zone of sharp focus in a photograph. With a shallow depth of field, the subject on which you focus is sharp but surrounding objects become progressively less sharp as their distance from the subject increases. With a large depth of field, the distance at which objects begin to blur increases.

digital zoom: An in-camera software process that attempts to mimic a real zoom lens, but in reality simply crops the perimeter of the image and then enlarges the area at the center, reducing image quality. Also does not generate the same optical results as a real zoom lens, which produces a change in perspective and depth of field as you zoom.

Glossary of Digital Photography Terms *(continued)*

diopter: A lens attachment that increases the camera's close-focusing distance, allowing extreme close-ups.

DNG: Stands for *Digital Negative.* A new imaging file format developed by Adobe Systems to address the fact that each camera manufacturer has developed its own, proprietary flavor of the Camera Raw format. DNG is offered as a potential new Raw-capture standard.

dpi: Short for *dots per inch,* a value that specifies how many dots of color a printer can lay down per linear inch. Often confused with *ppi,* or *pixels per inch,* which is a measurement of camera resolution.

dynamic autofocus: A focus mode in which the camera attempts to adjust focus as needed to track a moving object.

E

edge: An area where a significant color or brightness shift occurs between neighboring pixels. (The border between a light sky and a dark foreground is an edge, for example.)

EV (exposure value) compensation: Found on most digital cameras, a control that allows you to override the exposure chosen by a camera's autoexposure system. An EV compensation setting of 0.0 applies no exposure adjustment; a positive value produces a brighter exposure; and a negative value produces a darker exposure. Typically indicated by a plus/minus (+/−) sign in camera menus and displays.

EXIF metadata: Extra data that a camera stores with an image file. Includes data about the camera settings used to capture the picture, the date, and camera model. You can view this data in many image-cataloging and photo-editing programs. EXIF stands for *Exchangeable Image File Format.*

F

feathering: An option available when creating a selection outline in a photo editor. When an outline is feathered, the subsequent edit to the picture fades in gradually at the edges of the outline.

file format: A specific method of organizing and storing the data that comprises a digital picture file. The three most common digital camera formats are JPEG, TIFF, and Camera Raw.

fill flash: A flash setting that forces the flash to fire regardless of lighting conditions. Also known as *force flash.*

firmware: Built into a digital camera, the internal software that controls the camera's performance. Some manufacturer Web sites post firmware updates that address errors in the original firmware or simply enhance the performance of a particular camera feature. Users can then download and install the update into their cameras.

fixed-focus lens: A lens that has focus permanently set at the factory so that it is focused at an "average" midrange picture-taking distance. Sometimes referred to as a *focus-free lens.*

flash EV compensation: Similar to EV compensation, but adjusts the strength of the camera's flash instead of altering the exposure.

focal length: A measurement of the distance between the center of a camera lens and the recording medium (film negative or image sensor). Measured in millimeters; determines the area that the lens can "see," the size of the subject with respect to surrounding objects, and the apparent depth of field. Because focal length depends on the size of the recording medium, and because no standard sensor size exists for digital cameras, digital focal lengths are stated in terms of the equivalent focal length on a camera that uses a 35mm film negative.

force flash: *See* fill flash.

f-stop or f-number: The number that indicates the size of the camera aperture; stated as f/2, f/5.6, and so on. A higher number indicates a smaller aperture, which permits less light to strike the image sensor. A higher f-stop also produces greater depth of field. *(See Chapter 2 illustration.)*

G

gamut: Another word for *spectrum.* Refers to the range of colors that an imaging device can produce. Pronounced *gam-mutt.* Colors that a device can't create are said to be *out of gamut.*

Gaussian blur: Found in many photo-editing programs, an effects filter that blurs an image. Named after the mathematician Karl Gauss.

grayscale: An image that contains only black, white, and shades of gray; what most people commonly refer to as a black-and-white image.

H

histogram: A graph that indicates the distribution of highlights, shadows, and midtones in an image. Some cameras can display a histogram in the monitor to enable the photographer to evaluate exposure. Also found in some exposure-correction dialog boxes. *(See Chapter 2 illustration.)*

I

image stabilization: Found in some digital cameras, a feature designed to compensate for small amounts of camera shake. Also known as *antishake* or *vibration reduction.*

ISO: Stands for International Standards Organization and refers to the light sensitivity of film or a digital image sensor. Most digital cameras enable the user to choose from several ISO settings. A higher ISO enables the photographer to capture an image with less light but also increases the chance of noise, a defect that gives the image a speckled appearance. *(See Chapter 1 illustration.)*

J

JPEG: The default file format on most digital cameras; pronounced *jay-peg.* Also the best format for any online use and for multimedia presentations. But JPEG applies lossy compression, which damages image quality when applied to a high degree. *(See Chapter 1 illustration.)*

JPEG optimizer: A software tool that provides previews to help the user find the right balance of image quality and file size when preparing JPEG images for online use.

K

Kelvin: The scientific scale used to measure the color temperature of light; named for the physicist who developed it. Temperatures are stated as 5,000 Kelvin,

without the word *degree* or the degree symbol.

kilobyte: A unit of computer data equaling 1,000 bytes. Abbreviated as *K,* as in 64K. *See also* byte.

L

LCD: Stands for *liquid crystal display.* The type of technology used on most digital camera monitors.

Levels filter: An exposure-correction filter found in many photo-editing programs. This filter enables the user to manipulate shadows, highlights, and midtones separately.

lossless compression: A type of file compression that eliminates only redundant data, which preserves image quality but results in larger file sizes than lossy compression. Typically applied when a file is saved in the TIFF format.

lossy compression: A compression scheme that is less discriminating about eliminating image data than lossless compression. Applied when a file is saved in the JPEG format; sometimes also simply called JPEG compression. High amounts of lossy compression reduce image quality. *(See Chapter 1 illustration.)*

M

macro mode: Close-up focusing mode; usually indicated by a flower symbol on camera dials and menus.

marching ants: *See* selection outline.

marquee: *See* selection outline.

masking: A photo-editing process that protects part of an image from being affected by any changes. *See also* selecting.

matrix metering: *See* pattern metering.

megabyte: One million bytes. Abbreviated as MB. *See also* bit.

megapixel: One million pixels. Sometimes abbreviated as mp.

Memory Stick: A type of memory card used by many imaging and multimedia products manufactured by Sony.

Glossary of Digital Photography Terms *(continued)*

metadata: Data such as image-capture information (exposure settings, focal length, ISO, and so on) that is stored in an image file. *See also* EXIF metadata.

metering mode: A specific formula used by a camera's autoexposure system to determine the correct shutter speed and aperture. Each mode calculates exposure based on a different area of the frame. Depending on the scene, changing the metering mode produces a different exposure. *See also* spot metering, center-weighted metering, pattern metering.

midtones: Areas of medium brightness in a photograph.

MultiMediaCard (MMC): A type of camera memory card.

multispot autofocus: An autofocus zone in which the camera attempts to find a focus point that is appropriate for the majority of objects in the frame.

multizone metering: *See* pattern metering.

N

neutral density filter: A lens filter that reduces the amount of light that passes through the lens without altering colors.

noise: A defect that gives an image a speckled look, similar to film grain. Can be caused by dim lighting, a high ISO setting, a very long exposure, or a blip in the electrical signal generated during the image-capture process. Noise comes in two forms: *luminance* noise, which appears as monochrome speckling; and *color* noise, which looks a little like colored confetti. *(See Chapter 1 illustration.)*

nondestructive file format: A format that does not apply lossy compression or otherwise reduce image quality. TIFF and PSD (the Photoshop Elements format) are both nondestructive formats.

O

optical zoom: A true zoom lens (as opposed to digital zoom), which enables the photographer to capture a scene at several different focal lengths with the same lens. Zooming changes the size of the subject in the frame, the angle of view, and the apparent depth of field.

output resolution: Refers to the number of pixels per linear inch (ppi) in a printed photo. This term does not apply for on-screen images. If printing via photo-editing software, the user sets the output resolution prior to sending the image to the printer. When an image is printed directly from a memory card or camera, the printer or camera establishes the output resolution.

P

pattern metering: An autoexposure mode that bases the exposure on the entire frame; also known as *matrix, average,* or *multizone* metering.

pixels: The tiny squares of color that comprise the basic building block of a digital image. Pixels are similar to tiles in a mosaic. *(See Chapter 1 illustration.)*

platform: Refers to the operating system used by a computer (for example, the Microsoft Windows platform or the Macintosh platform).

plug-in: An add-on computer program that extends the capabilities of another, usually larger, program. Many special-effects plug-ins are available for Adobe Photoshop, Photoshop Elements, and other popular imaging software.

ppi: A measurement of image output resolution; stands for *pixels per inch* (but measures pixels per linear inch, not square inch). Applies only to printed photos and plays a large role in print quality. *See also* output resolution.

R

Raw: *See* Camera Raw.

Raw converter: A program used to translate the data from a Camera Raw image file into an actual picture and create a copy of the file in a standard format that photo-editing programs can read. Required to open or edit Raw files. Most cameras that offer the Camera Raw format ship with a converter. Many photo-editing programs, including Photoshop Elements, also offer this tool.

red-eye reduction flash: A flash mode designed to reduce the chances of red eye. The camera emits a small preflash before the real flash to cause the subject's pupils to contract.

resampling: The process of adding or deleting image pixels in a photo editor. Too much resampling degrades images, especially when adding pixels. *(See Chapter 1 illustration.)*

resolution: In general, a measurement of how finely an imaging device can render a photo or graphic. Specific resolution values indicate different things depending on the device.

RGB: Stands for *red, green, blue.* A generic color model used by all devices that produce images by mixing light (digital cameras, scanners, monitors, and televisions). *See also* color model.

S

saturation: The intensity of purity of a color. A fully saturated color contains no black, white, or gray.

scene modes: Available on some digital cameras, these special capture modes automatically select settings appropriate for specific types of pictures, such as portraits, landscapes, or sports shots. Also known as *creative scene modes.*

SD Card: Short for *Secure Digital.* A type of camera memory card.

selectable zone autofocus: An autofocus mode in which the photographer can select from several areas of the frame on which to establish focus.

selecting: A photo-editing process that enables the user to apply a change only to certain parts of an image. This process is similar to highlighting text before applying a change in a word-processing program.

selection outline: In a photo-editing program, the dotted outline that appears to indicate what parts of an image are selected and will be affected by the next filter or tool the user applies. Also known as a *marquee* and *marching ants.*

sharpening: A software filter that creates the illusion of sharper focus by increasing contrast along color and brightness boundaries (edges). *See also* Unsharp Mask filter.

shutter: A barrier between the image sensor and aperture. When the shutter button is pressed, the shutter opens briefly to allow light to pass through the aperture and strike the sensor. *(See Chapter 2 illustration.)*

shutter-priority autoexposure: A semi-automatic exposure mode. You select the shutter speed, and the camera automatically chooses the right aperture to expose the image properly. Useful for controlling whether moving objects appear blurred in an image. Typically indicated on a camera dial by the letters *S* or *Tv* (for *time value*).

shutter speed: The length of time that the shutter is open when the shutter button is pressed. Measured in fractions of a second, such as 1/60 second. Determines whether moving objects appear blurry in the image.

slave flash: A standalone flash unit that fires automatically in response to the light of the camera's main flash.

slow-synch flash: Available on some cameras, a flash setting that synchronizes the shutter and flash at a slower speed than normal flash. The background is then lit by ambient light; the foreground, by the flash. Produces brighter backgrounds in nighttime pictures, but can result in subject blurring due to the slower shutter speed.

SmartMedia: A memory card used primarily in older model digital cameras; no longer used in new models.

spot metering: An autoexposure mode that bases exposure only on the center of the frame.

sRGB: A variation on the RGB color model. Defines a more limited color spectrum that includes only those colors that most cameras, monitors, scanners, and printers can reproduce. Stands for *standard RGB. (See Chapter 1 illustration.)*

stop down the aperture: To select a higher f-stop, which results in a smaller aperture.

T

TIFF: Short for *tagged image file format* and pronounced *tiff,* as in spat. Along with JPEG and Camera Raw, TIFF is one of three common formats for digital camera files. Applies lossless compression, which retains all

Glossary of Digital Photography Terms *(continued)*

critical image data but creates substantially larger files than JPEG. This format is good for saving files after you edit them in a photo editor and is compatible with most word-processing and page-layout programs, but it isn't readable by e-mail programs or Web browsers.

TWAIN driver: A small bit of software code that sometimes must be installed on a computer in order for the computer to communicate with a digital camera or scanner. Manufacturers whose products require the TWAIN driver include it on the software CD that ships in the camera box.

U

Unsharp Mask filter: A common photo-editing filter used to create the illusion of a more sharply focused image. Named after a traditional darkroom technique and sometimes abbreviated as USM filter. *(See Chapter 3 illustration.)*

USB: Short for *Universal Serial Bus.* A type of port for connecting digital cameras and other devices to a computer.

W

warming filter: A color filter placed over the camera lens to add a warm, gold cast to an image.

Web-safe color: One of 256 colors included in a standard palette that incorporates only those colors that the majority of computer monitors and video cards can display.

white balancing: A digital camera feature that neutralizes the color casts produced by various light sources. *(See Chapter 4 illustration.)*

wide-gamut color space: A generic term describing a color space that includes more colors than the sRGB space, which has a limited gamut.

X

xD-Picture Card: A type of memory card used in some digital cameras. It is smaller than a postage stamp.

Symbol Quick Reference

The table below offers a quick guide to symbols commonly used to indicate various camera controls. Keep in mind that the symbols shown here are generic; the actual symbols on your camera may appear slightly different.

Control	Symbol	Control	Symbol
Program autoexposure	 📷 AUTO	Auto flash	 ⚡ AUTO
Manual exposure	M	Fill (or force) flash	 ⚡
Aperture-priority autoexposure	A or Av	Red-eye reduction	👁
Shutter-priority autoexposure	S or Tv	Fill flash with red-eye reduction	 ⚡ 👁
EV compensation	 ±🔲	No flash	 🚫⚡
Whole-frame metering (pattern, average, multispot, matrix)	 ▦	Flash EV compensation	 ⚡ ±🔲
Center-weighted metering	 ⊙	White Balance	WB
Spot metering	 ▫	Cloudy	 ☁
Macro focus	 🌷	Sunny	 ☀
Landscape scene mode	 ⛰	Incandescent	 💡
Portrait scene mode	 👤	Fluorescent	 💡
Action scene mode	 🚶	Self-timer	 ⏱
Nighttime scene mode	 🌙★		

Products/Services Quick Reference

For more information about products and services mentioned in this book, visit these Web sites:

Product/Service	Company/Web Address
Adobe Photoshop Elements	Adobe Systems (www.adobe.com)
Color management products	ColorVision (www.colorvision.com)
	GretagMacbeth (www.gretagmacbeth.com)
	X-Rite (www.xrite.com)
Drawing tablets	Wacom Technology (www.wacom.com)
Lighting equipment	Cloud Dome, Inc. (www.clouddome.com)
	Lastolite Limited (www.lastolite.com)
	Lowel (www.lowel.com)
	Photoflex (www.photoflex.com)
	Smith-Victor (www.smithvictor.com)
Online photo sharing/printing	Fujifilm USA (www.digitalcameradeveloping.com)
	Kodak Gallery (www.kodakgallery.com)
	Prints Are Memories (www.prints-are-memories.com)
	Shutterfly (www.shutterfly.com)
	Snapfish (www.snapfish.com)
Retailers (photography hardware and software)	B&H Photo Video (www.bhphotovideo.com)
	Calumet Photographic (www.calumetphoto.com)
	Roberts Imaging (www.robertsimaging.com)
	Samy's Camera (www.samys.com)
Tripods	Bogen Imaging (www.bogenimaging.com)
	Joby, Inc. (www.joby.com)

My Camera Quick Reference

For each feature, note the specific options available on your camera as well as how to access them. If your camera doesn't offer a feature, just leave the My Camera column blank.

Feature	My Camera
Resolution	

File format	
☐ JPEG	
☐ TIFF	
☐ Camera Raw	

ISO	
☐ Auto	
☐ Manual	

Digital zoom	

Exposure modes	
☐ Manual exposure	
☐ Program autoexposure (AE)	
☐ Aperture-priority AE	
☐ Shutter-priority AE	

EV compensation	

Autoexposure metering modes	
☐ Whole-frame metering (pattern, matrix, multispot, average, and so on)	
☐ Center-weighted metering	
☐ Spot metering	

Autofocus zones	
☐ Center-area	
☐ Closest-subject	
☐ Continuous (dynamic)	
☐ Other	

My Camera Quick Reference *(continued)*

Feature	*My Camera*
Macro focus	

Scene modes

☐ Portrait

☐ Landscape

☐ Action (or Sports)

☐ Nighttime

☐ Other

White Balance

☐ Auto

☐ Manual

Flash

☐ Auto

☐ Fill (or force)

☐ Red-eye reduction

☐ No flash

☐ Flash EV compensation

In-camera image adjustments

☐ Saturation

☐ Sharpening

☐ Sepia/black-and-white

Self-timer

Review images

Delete images

Format memory card (erases all images)

Set Up Color Management in Photoshop Elements

Photoshop Elements offers several color management options that help ensure color consistency. The remainder of this appendix explains how to implement these features, which is a four-part process.

If you're new to the subject of color management, read the Chapter 1 section related to color spaces before you start so that you can better understand the instructions found here.

I. Tell the program to ignore EXIF color profile data.

Every picture file that your camera creates includes some extra data, known as *EXIF metadata (x-if met-ah-date-ah)*. This data records camera settings such as aperture, shutter speed, ISO, and most important to this discussion, color profile. You can view the metadata in some image browsers; in the Elements Organizer (Windows only), click a thumbnail and then choose Window⇨Properties to display the window shown to the right.

By default, Elements looks first to the metadata to determine the image color profile. For reasons I won't bore you with, the color-profile metadata code generated by some cameras sometimes indicates sRGB even when the actual profile is Adobe RGB. (See Chapter 1 for an explanation of sRGB and Adobe RGB.) To be safe, tell Elements *not* to take profile information from the EXIF data. Here's how:

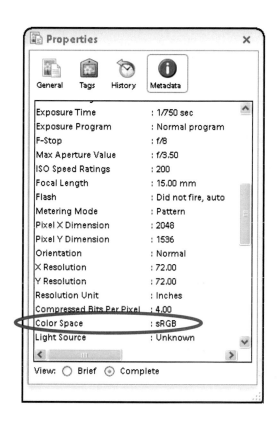

Set Up Color Management in Photoshop Elements *(continued)*

❶ Open the Preferences dialog box.

In Windows, choose Edit➪Preferences➪ Saving Files. On a Mac, choose Photoshop Elements➪Preferences➪Saving Files.

❷ Select the Ignore Camera Data (EXIF) Profiles box.

I circled the box in the figure to the right.

❸ Click OK to close the dialog box.

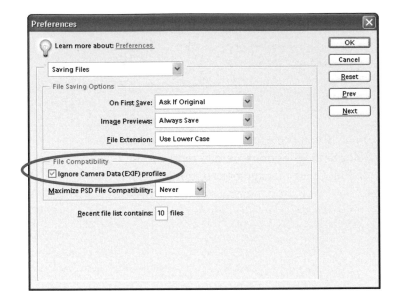

II. Turn on color management in the Color Settings dialog box.

Follow these steps:

❶ Open the Color Settings dialog box.

In Windows, choose Edit➪Color Settings; on a Mac, choose Photoshop Elements➪ Color Settings. You see the dialog box shown to the right.

❷ Specify Adobe RGB as your preferred color profile.

The options in this dialog box control what color profile Elements uses to open and display your images if no color profile is already attached to the file. You can select either Adobe RGB or sRGB.

As I explain in Chapter 1, I prefer Adobe RGB to sRGB because it allows a broader color palette. To choose Adobe RGB as your

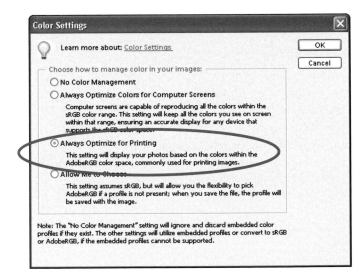

default profile, select the Always Optimize for Printing option and click OK. Now when you open an image that has no profile, the program assigns the Adobe RGB profile. If you open a picture that has some other profile, the program respects that profile if possible; if not, the picture is converted to Adobe RGB.

Note: If you still use Elements 3.0, your Color Settings options are different; choose the Full Color Management option. If you see a Missing Profile dialog box when you open an image, select Assign Adobe RGB and click OK.

❸ Click OK.

III. When you save an image after editing, embed the profile.

Embedding the profile simply means storing the profile information with the file. If you later open the image in a program that supports color profiles, the program will know what profile to use. Follow these steps to embed the profile when saving an image:

❶ Choose File⇨Save As to open the Save As dialog box.

❷ Select the option to embed the profile.

In Windows, select the option named ICC Profile (circled in the figure to the right). On a Mac, the option is named Embed Color Profile.

Do *not* embed profiles when saving files in the JPEG format for use on the Internet. Embedding the profile adds to the file size,

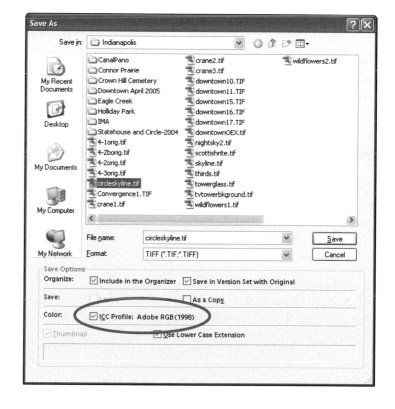

and most Web browsers and e-mail programs can't read the profiles anyway.

③ Click OK to close the dialog box and save the file.

IV. When you print, specify the output (printer) profile.

When you choose the Print command in Elements (File➪Print), you see the Print Preview dialog box. Follow these steps to set the color-management options in this dialog box:

① Select the Show More Options box to uncover the color-management options.

These options are circled in the figure to the right.

(The File Name, Caption, and Transfer Printing options are not related to color management. They control other features that might come in handy for some print jobs. See the Elements Help system for information on what they do.)

② Select a printer profile from the Printer Profile drop-down list.

The Source Space item in the Print Preview dialog box shows the color profile of your image. You select a printer profile from the Printer Profile list, as shown in the figure to the right.

When you installed your printer, the printer software likely installed one or more generic profiles. To locate them, open the Printer Profiles list. Many printers install

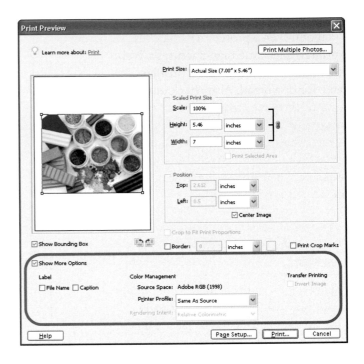

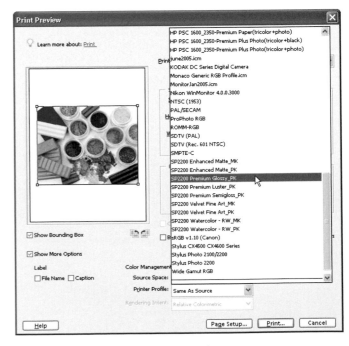

multiple profiles, each characterizing how the machine outputs colors on a specific paper stock. For example, on my Epson printer, there are profiles for printing on glossy stock, matte paper, and so on. Select the profile that most closely matches your paper.

If you don't see a profile that matches your printer, check the manufacturer's Web site. Many manufacturers make profiles available for download. Also check out the Web site of the paper manufacturer. More and more paper manufacturers are posting profiles for their specialty photo papers to help photographers achieve better results. Follow the instructions on the Web sites to download and install the profiles.

❸ Set the Rendering Intent option to Perceptual or Relative Colormetric.

The Rendering Intent option just gives the program some additional information on how to interpret color data. In most cases, Perceptual or Relative Colormetric work best for photos, but experiment with your printer.

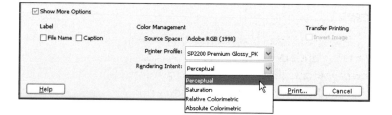

Index

Numerics

8-bit images, 18
16-bit images, 18
81 series filters, 112

A

Action scene mode
  effect on shutter speed, 51, 96
  symbol, 49, 96, 193
  zoo photography example, 171, 172
Adobe Gamma, 28, 29
Adobe Photoshop Elements 4.0
  alternatives to, 31
  aspect ratio options, 140, 142, 143
  brush-based tools, 32–35
  Color Picker tool, 36, 113
  Color Variations filter, 113, 114–116
  computer monitor profiling, 28–29
  converting images from Camera Raw to another file
    format, 17–22
  creating blurry background, 83–85, 175
  cursor options, 35
  Hue/Saturation filter, 115, 119, 120–121, 130,
    168–169, 176
  inappropriate print size warning, 13
  Info palette, 139–141, 142, 143
  Photo Filter tool, 113, 114, 169
  Print Preview dialog box, 13, 200
  producing grayscale images, 127–128
  producing sepia-toned images, 129–130
  Reduce Noise filter, 150–152
  saving images for Web, 153–157
  setting up color management, 197–201
  Shadows/Highlights filter, 73–74, 167
  straightening tilted images, 134–135
  toolbox overview, 30–45
  tweaking exposure, 69–72
Adobe RGB
  as color management tool, 29, 197, 198–199
  defined, 184
  description, 24–25
  versus sRGB, 24–25
AE. See autoexposure (AE)
airbrush mode, 34

aliasing, defined, 184. See also anti-aliasing
animals, photographing, 170–176
anti-aliasing
  defined, 184
  illustrated, 45
  selecting, 45, 137
antique-looking images, 129–130
antishake feature, digital cameras, 87
aperture
  adjusting for indoor portraits, 59
  defined, 48, 49, 184
  in Landscape scene mode, 50, 94, 95
  in Portrait scene mode, 50, 57, 80, 162
  for product shots, 180–181
  relationship to depth of field, 49, 50, 79
  relationship to f-stops, 79–80, 94
  relationship to shutter speed, 48–49, 51, 80
  setting, 49
aperture-priority autoexposure
  alternatives to, 80
  applying EV compensation, 55, 160
  defined, 49, 184
  switching to, 162
  symbol, 49, 193
  waterfall image example, 99
Apple Macintosh computers
  Adobe Bridge, 13
  color management options, 198, 199
  cursor options, 35
  Display Calibrator Assistant, 28
  monitor profiling, 28, 29
  on-screen photographs, 75
artifacts
  defined, 184
  minimizing with JPEG camera settings, 14–15
  removing in Photoshop Elements, 151
aspect ratios
  defined, 184
  film versus digital images, 26
  framing images for print flexibility, 26
  Photoshop Elements options, 140, 142, 143
auto flash symbol, 193
autoexposure (AE). See also aperture-priority
    autoexposure; shutter-priority autoexposure
  applying EV compensation, 54–55, 160
  changing metering mode, 52–53, 161

autoexposure (AE) *(continued)*
  defined, 49, 184
  shutter button technique, 51, 89, 92, 93
  symbols, 49, 193
autofocus
  baboon image example, 172–173
  caution when shooting through glass, 171
  center-area, 91–92, 93, 172
  close-up mode, 90, 100
  closest-object, 93
  continuous, 89
  dynamic, 93
  faking out, 92
  how to lock in focus, 51, 89, 92, 93
  image troubleshooting, 89–93
  and lens focusing range, 90
  macro mode, 90, 100
  multispot, 93
  overview, 91–93
  selectable zone, 92
  shooting through glass, 171
  shutter button technique, 51, 89, 92, 93
  troubleshooting, 90–93
autofocus zones
  camera options, 92–93
  defined, 91, 184
  description, 91
average metering, 52. *See also* pattern metering

B

baboon image example, 170–176
background
  blurring in photo editor, 83–85
  busy, avoiding, 161
  copying to new layer, 84
  quick reference, 191
  softening by shortening depth of field, 78–82, 162
background paint color, 36, 37
backlighting, 160–161, 165
banding, 18, 184
bit depth, 18, 184
bits, defined, 18, 184
black, 131. *See also* CMYK color model
black-and-white *versus* color, 127–128
blending mode, 33, 125, 126
blue, 131. *See also* RGB color model
blur
  baboon image example, 175
  using to diminish noise, 150–152
  using to soften background, 83–85, 175

blurry pictures, avoiding, 86–88, 191
bracketing, 63, 99, 184
brightness. *See also* contrast
  adjusting in Raw converter, 19, 20
  effect of camera settings, 49
  improving low-light landscapes, 166–169
  increasing, 160–161, 191
  in print *versus* on screen, 75
Brush tool
  airbrush mode, 34
  customizing, 32–35
  Hardness value, 35
  keyboard shortcuts, 32
  Mode control, 33
  Opacity value, 33
  red-eye repair example, 125–126
  setting options, 32–33
Brushes palette
  Aligned option, 146–147
  customizing tools, 32–35
  Mode control, 33, 146
  Opacity value, 33, 146
  overview, 32, 145
  Sample All Layers option, 148
  Size control, 32, 145
bulbs, photoflood, 65, 66
bytes, defined, 11, 184

C

camera monitors
  as digital camera feature, 87
  versus viewfinders, 86
  viewing white balance settings, 111
Camera Raw format. *See also* Raw converter
  advantages, 16
  converting to another file format, 17–22
  defined, 16, 184
  disadvantages, 16–17
  file size issues, 16–17
  saving converted images, 22
  shooting pictures in, 16–17
  when to create JPEG copies, 179
cameras. *See* digital cameras
Canvas Size dialog box, 136
CCDs (charge-coupled devices), defined, 184
CcMmYK color model, defined, 185
center-area autofocus, 91–92, 93, 172, 193
center-weighted metering
  defined, 52, 184
  versus pattern metering, 161

symbol, 52, 193
when to use, 53
charge-coupled devices (CCDs), defined, 184
clipped highlights, 17, 20, 185
clipped shadows, 17, 20, 185
clone sources, defined, 146
Clone tool
  Aligned option, 146–147
  baboon image example, 174
  defined, 144, 185
  Sample-All-Layers option, 148
  using, 144, 145, 148
close-up filters. *See* diopters
closest-object autofocus, 93, 185
Cloud Dome, 66, 68
Cloudy symbol, 113, 164, 165, 193
CMOS (complementary metal-oxide semiconductor),
    defined, 185
CMS (color-management system), 29, 185
CMYK color model, defined, 185
color balancing, 114–116
color blooming, defined, 118
color cast. *See* white balance
color channels, 18, 185
color images
  converting to grayscale images, 127–128
  converting to sepia-toned images, 129–130
  prints *versus* on-screen, 10–11, 75, 131
color-management system (CMS), 29, 185
color matching, 131
color models, 24–25, 185
color noise
  defined, 21, 151
  illustrated, 21
  reducing in Raw converter, 21
  reducing with Reduce Noise filter, 151
Color Picker tool, 36, 113
color profiles
  customizing, 28–29
  defined, 28, 185
  embedding, 199–201
color saturation. *See* saturation
color space. *See* color models
color spectrum. *See* gamut
color temperature, 110, 111, 185. *See also* Kelvin
Color Variations filter, 113, 114–116
color wheel, 114, 115
colorimeters, 29, 185
ColorMatch RGB, 25
colors, Web-safe, 37. *See also* paint colors
CompactFlash, defined, 185

complementary metal-oxide semiconductor (CMOS),
    defined, 185
compression
  balancing image quality with file size in Web-friendly
    JPEG images, 156
  defined, 185
  versus image quality, 14–15
  lossy, 14, 15, 149
computer monitors
  pressure-sensitive tablets for, 34
  versus printed pictures, 10–11, 75, 131
  profiling, 28–29
connection speed, setting, 154
Contiguous control, Magic Wand, 43–44
continuous autofocus, 89, 185
contrast
  adjusting in Raw converter, 19, 20
  high, adjusting by using Shadows/Highlights filter,
    73–74
  increasing by using Levels filter, 176
convergence, 136–138, 185
cooler images, 58, 61, 111
creative scene modes. *See* scene modes
cropping. *See also* aspect ratios
  Crop tool *versus* Crop command, 173
  drawbacks of digital zoom, 23
  effect of digital zoom, 171
  to eliminate excess background, 173
  to improve image composition, 139–141
  increasing resolution for, 12
  planning for, 163
  product image example, 181
  saving images, 141
  to specific dimensions, 142–143
CRW file format, 17
cursor options, 35
cyan, 131. *See also* CMYK color model

D

depth of field (DOF)
  defined, 49, 185
  extending, 94–95, 172
  in Landscape scene mode, 192
  in product shots, 180, 181
  relationship to aperture, 49, 50, 79
  relationship to focal length, 81, 94
  shortening, 78–82, 162
  ways to adjust, 78–82
diffuser umbrellas, 67, 68
diffusing lights, 66–67

digital cameras
  antishake feature, 87
  aspect ratio, 26
  autofocus zones, 92–93
  automated red-eye removal, 123
  avoiding blur, 86–88
  file format overview, 14–17
  framing images, 26–27
  hand-holding, 86
  image stabilization feature, 87
  instant playback feature, 97
  lens focus range, 90
  monitors *versus* viewfinders, 86
  My Camera quick reference, 195–196
  picture makeover quick reference, 191–192
  pressing shutter button, 51, 89, 92, 93
  saturation control, 118–119
  scene modes, 49, 193
  self-timer mode, 88
  setting resolution, 10–11, 12
  steadying, 86–88
  tips for shooting portraits, 165
  tripods for, 87
  turning off flash, 57, 64, 98
  vibration reduction feature, 87
  viewfinder location, 27
  zoom options, 23, 80–81
digital negative. *See* DNG format
digital prints
  black-and-white, 128
  versus on-screen images, 10–11, 75, 131
  preserving, 121
  retail options, 165
digital zoom
  defined, 23, 185
  versus optical zoom, 23, 81
  turning off, 23, 171
diopters, 101, 186
Display Calibrator Assistant, 28, 29
displays. *See* camera monitors; computer monitors
DNG format, 22, 186
DOF. *See* depth of field (DOF)
dots per inch (dpi), defined, 186
dpi (dots per inch), defined, 186
dynamic autofocus, 93. *See also* continuous autofocus

E

edges. *See also* sharpening
  brush options for, 34–35, 39–41, 175
  defined, 45, 186
  selecting anti-aliasing option, 45, 137

embedding color profiles, 199–201
Eraser tool, 84, 106, 148
EV (exposure value) compensation
  applying, 54–55, 63
  applying to sunset portraits, 63
  defined, 54, 186
  symbol, 54, 193
  when to use higher value, 55, 161
  when to use lower value, 54, 55, 161
Exchangeable Image File Format. *See* EXIF metadata
EXIF metadata, 186, 197, 198
exposure. *See also* autoexposure (AE); manual-exposure mode
  adjusting in Raw converter, 19–20
  bracketing, 63, 99
  changing autoexposure metering mode, 52–53, 161
  control modes, 49
  long, in waterfall image example, 98–99
  overview, 48–49
  quick reference, 191
  tips for sunset portraits, 62–63
  tweaking in photo editor program, 69–72
exposure value. *See* EV (exposure value) compensation
Eyedropper tool, 36–37, 125

F

f-numbers. *See* f-stops
f-stops. *See also* aperture
  defined, 48, 186
  higher *versus* lower, 79–80, 94
  relationship to aperture, 79–80
feathering, 175, 186
file formats
  Camera Raw, 16–22, 179
  converting Camera Raw to another format, 17–22
  defined, 14, 186
  DNG, 22, 186
  JPEG, 14–15, 149, 151, 153, 155–156, 178–179
  PSD, 15, 22, 42, 149
  TIFF, 15, 16, 22, 42, 149, 179
fill flash
  defined, 61, 186
  symbol, 193
  using in outdoor portraits, 60–61, 62, 163
film cameras
  aspect ratio, 26
  focal length values, 95
filters
  warming, 113, 164
firmware, defined, 186
fixed-focus lenses, 91, 186

flash
   avoiding in indoor portraits, 56–59
   avoiding in product shots, 64, 179–180
   blocking, 98
   changing from automatic mode, 61
   external flash heads, 65
   lighting alternatives, 65–68
   quick reference, 191
   reducing occurrence red eye, 62, 122–123
   slave units, 65
   symbols, 193
   turning off, 57, 64, 98
   using outdoors, 60–61, 62, 163
flash EV compensation, 186, 193
Flatten Image option, 85, 107, 126, 149
flower icon. *See* macro mode
Fluorescent symbol, 193
focal length
   defined, 80, 186
   digital *versus* film camera values, 95
   how it is measured, 95
   increasing by zooming in, 80–81, 162
   relationship to depth of field, 81, 94
   shortening by zooming out, 94
focus. *See also* autofocus
   checking in through-the-lens viewfinder, 101
   manual, 92
   quick reference, 191
   range of lens, 90
   relationship to shutter speed, 49, 50–51
   sharpening in Photoshop Elements, 102–107
focus-free lenses, 91
force flash. *See* fill flash
foreground paint color, 36, 37
"freezing" objects, 96–97, 191

G

Gamma. *See* Adobe Gamma
gamut, 24–25, 186
Gaussian blur filter, 84, 175, 187
glass, shooting through, 171
grayscale, 127–128, 187
green, 131. *See also* RGB color model
green eye, repairing, 124–126

H

Hand tool, 31
handles, defined, 134

hardness, brush, 35, 39–40, 41
high-contrast images, 73–74
highlights
   adjusting in Levels filter, 70, 71, 72, 168
   adjusting in Raw converter, 19, 20
   exposing for, 73
   in high-contrast images, 73–74
   toning down by using Shadows/Highlights filter, 74, 167
histograms
   defined, 70, 187
Hue/Saturation filter
   versus Color Variations filter, 115
   desaturating colors, 120–121, 176
   increasing saturation, 119, 168–169, 176
   making sepia-toned images, 130

I

ICC Profile option, 156, 199
image profiles, embedding, 199–201
image stabilization, 87, 187
Incandescent symbol, 193
indoor portraits, avoiding use of flash, 56–59
Info palette, 139, 140–141, 142, 143
inkjet printers, making black-and-white prints on, 128
International Standards Organization. *See* ISO
Internet, specifying connection speed, 154
ISO
   adjusting for indoor portraits, 59
   adjusting setting, 8–9, 48, 49
   camera Auto setting, 9
   defined, 48, 49, 187
   relationship to noise, 8–9, 49, 63

J

JPEG format
   advantages, 14
   versus Camera Raw format, 16–17
   compression *versus* image quality, 14–15
   as default, 14
   defined, 14, 187
   disadvantages, 14
   for product shots, 178–179
   reducing artifacts, 14–15, 151
   shooting pictures in, 14–15
   ways to save edited images, 15
   for Web-friendly images, 153, 155–156
   when to use, 149, 153
JPEG optimizer, 153–157, 187

K

Kelvin, 110, 111, 113, 187
kilobytes, defined, 11, 187
Kodak Gallery, 164

L

lamps, professional-grade, 65–66, 68
Landscape scene mode
    effect on aperture, 50, 94, 95
    effect on depth of field, 172
    symbol, 94, 193
    zoo photography example, 172
landscapes, low-light example, 166–169
layers
    adding for cloning pixels, 144
    adding for fixing red eye, 125–126
    duplicating, 103
    Opacity value, 106
    sampling, 45, 148
LCDs (liquid crystal displays), defined, 187
lens flare, 63
lenses
    fixed-focus, 91
    focal length values, 95
    focus-free, 91
    focusing range, 90
    hoods for, 63
    shift-tilt, 136
Levels filter
    adjusting exposure, 69–72, 115
    baboon image example, 176
    defined, 69, 187
    Highlights slider, 70, 71, 72, 168
    histogram, 70
    increasing contrast, 176
    low-light landscape example, 168
    Midtones slider, 70, 71, 72, 168, 176
    Shadows slider, 70, 71, 176
    steps in using, 70–72
light tents, 67, 180
lighting, artificial
    diffusing, 66–67
    equipment resources, 67
    multiple lamps, 68
    for product shots, 64–68, 179–180
    professional-grade lamps for, 65–66
lion statue example, 78, 79–81, 83–85

liquid crystal displays (LCDs), defined, 187
lossless compression, defined, 187
lossy compression, 14, 15, 149, 187
luminance noise
    defined, 21, 151
    illustrated, 21
    reducing in Raw converter, 21
    reducing with Reduce Noise filter, 151

M

Macintosh computers
    Adobe Bridge, 13
    color management options, 198, 199
    cursor options, 35
    Display Calibrator Assistant, 28
    monitor profiling, 28, 29
    on-screen photographs, 75
macro mode, 90, 100, 187, 193
magenta, 131. *See also* CMYK color model
Magic Wand tool, 43–45, 120
manual-exposure mode
    defined, 49
    symbol, 49, 193
    waterfall example, 98–99
    zoo photography example, 171–172
manual focus, 92
manual white balancing, 110–111
marching ants. *See* selection outlines
marquee. *See* selection outlines
masking
    adjusting display, 40
    baboon image example, 175
    creating, 40–41, 83
    defined, 38, 187
    lion image example, 83
    setting Hardness value, 39, 40, 41
    undoing, 41
megabytes, defined, 11, 187
megapixels, 11, 187
memory cards
    effect of picture resolution on, 11
    high-speed, 97
    Memory Stick, 187
    MultiMediaCard, 188
    SD Card, 189
    SmartMedia, 189
    xD-Picture Card, 190
Memory Stick, defined, 187
metadata, 188, 197–199

metering modes
   center-weighted, 52, 53, 161, 193
   defined, 52, 188
   overview, 52–53, 191
   pattern, 52, 161
   spot, 52, 53, 161, 193
   symbols, 52, 193
   whole-frame, 193
Microsoft Windows computers
   Adobe Gamma, 28, 29
   Camera Raw file extensions, 17
   color management options, 198, 199
   cursor options, 35
   monitor profiling, 28, 29
   on-screen photographs, 75
   Organizer, 13
midtones
   adjusting in Raw converter, 19, 20
   adjusting with Levels filter, 70, 71, 72, 168, 176
   adjusting with Shadows/Highlights filter, 74, 167
   defined, 20, 188
modems, specifying connection speed, 154
monitors, camera
   as digital camera feature, 87
   versus viewfinders, 86
   viewing white balance settings, 111
monitors, computer
   pressure-sensitive tablets for, 34
   versus printed images, 10–11, 75, 131
   profiling, 28–29
monument image example, 86–88
MultiMediaCard (MMC), defined, 188
multispot autofocus, 93, 188
multizone metering, 52. *See also* pattern metering
My Camera quick reference, 195–196

N

NEF file format, 17
neutral density filter, 99, 188
Nighttime scene mode, 98–99, 193
noise
   applying blur to diminish, 9, 21, 150–152
   causes of, 9, 21
   caution in sunset portraits, 63
   defined, 8, 188
   effect of ISO setting, 8–9, 49
   quick reference, 191
   reducing with Raw converter, 21
   reducing with Reduce Noise filter, 151
   when to use Unsharp Mask filter, 105
nondestructive file format, 149, 188

O

online photo printing services, 164
opacity, 33, 106, 146
optical zoom, defined, 23, 81, 188. *See also* digital zoom;
      zoom lenses
optimizer. *See* JPEG optimizer
outdoor portraits, role of fill flash, 60–61, 62, 163
output resolution, defined, 188. *See also* prints, resolution
      issues

P

paint colors
   background, 36, 37
   foreground, 36, 37
   selecting by using Color Picker, 36
   selecting by using Eyedropper, 36–37
   swapping foreground and background, 37
painting to create mask, 40–41, 83
parallax errors, 27
pattern metering
   defined, 52, 188
   versus other metering modes, 52, 161
   when to use, 52
photo editors. *See* Photoshop Elements 4.0
Photo Filter tool, 113, 114, 169
photoflood bulbs, 65, 66
Photoshop Elements 4.0
   alternatives to, 31
   aspect ratio options, 140, 142, 143
   brush-based tools, 32–35
   Color Picker tool, 36, 113
   Color Variations filter, 113, 114–116
   computer monitor profiling, 28–29
   converting images from Camera Raw to another file
      format, 17–22
   creating blurry background, 83–85
   cursor options, 35
   Hue/Saturation filter, 119, 120–121, 130, 168–169, 176
   inappropriate print size warning, 13
   Info palette, 139–141, 142, 143
   Photo Filter tool, 113, 114, 169
   Print Preview dialog box, 13, 200
   producing grayscale images, 127–128
   producing sepia-toned images, 129–130
   Reduce Noise filter, 150–152
   saving images for Web, 153–157
   setting up color management, 197–201
   Shadows/Highlights filter, 73–74, 167
   straightening tilted images, 134–135

Photoshop Elements 4.0 *(continued)*
  toolbox overview, 30–45
  tweaking exposure, 69–72
picture elements. *See* pixels
pixels
  blending, 33
  calculating print size requirements, 11, 13
  cropping considerations, 12
  defined, 10, 188
  displaying ppi in Photoshop Elements, 13
  edited *versus* original, 33
  as measure of camera resolution, 10–11, 12
  minimum ppi needed for printed photos, 10, 11
  printed *versus* on-screen pictures, 10–11
  in Web-friendly images, 154–155
platforms, defined, 188. *See also* Macintosh computers;
      Windows computers
plug-ins, defined, 188
Portrait scene mode
  effect on aperture, 50, 57, 80, 162
  effect on exposure, 59
  symbol, 80, 162, 193
portraits
  indoor, ways to avoid using flash, 56–59
  outdoor, role of fill flash, 60–61, 62, 163
  tips for shooting, 165
posterization. *See* banding
ppi (pixels per inch)
  calculating print size requirements, 11, 13
  defined, 10, 188
  displaying in Photoshop Elements, 13
  minimum needed for printed photos, 10, 11
  printed *versus* on-screen pictures, 10–11
pressure-sensitive tablets, 34
print longevity, 121
Print Preview dialog box, 13, 200
print size
  aspect ratio issue, 26–27
  calculating resolution, 10–13
  checking appropriateness before printing, 13
  cropping images to fit, 26–27
Printer Profile list, 200–201
printers
  inkjet, making black-and-white prints on, 128
  output *versus* on-screen images, 10–11, 75, 131
  troubleshooting color issues, 131
prints. *See also* print size
  black-and-white, 128
  digital, preserving, 121
  versus on-screen images, 10–11, 75, 131

resolution issues, 10–11, 12
retail options, 165
products
  improving images, 177–181
  lighting, 64–68, 180
  photographing, 64–68
profiles. *See* color profiles; computer monitors, profiling;
      Printer Profile list
programmed autoexposure. *See* autoexposure (AE)
ProPhoto RGB, 25
PSD (Photoshop) format, saving images in, 15, 22, 42, 149

R

Raw. *See* Camera Raw format
Raw converter. *See also* Camera Raw format
  default setting adjustments, 19–20
  defined, 16, 188
  exposure adjustment options, 19–20
  saving converted images, 22
  using, 16–22
Rectangular Marquee tool, 142–143
red, 131. *See also* RGB color model
red eye
  camera symbols, 193, 194
  defined, 122
  fill flash mode for reducing occurrence, 62, 122
  removing in Photoshop Elements, 124–126
  repairing, 124–126
  ways to lower chances, 122–123
  why it happens, 122
red-eye reduction flash, 62, 122, 188, 194
Red-Eye Removal tool, 124
Reduce Color Noise slider, 151
Reduce Noise filter, 150–152
reflectors, 58, 59, 164
Remove Color Cast tool, 117
Rendering Intent option, 201
resampling, 13, 189
resolution
  calculating print size requirements, 11
  defined, 10, 189
  digital camera settings, 10–11, 12
  effect on cropped images, 12
  versus file size, 11
  high, using for zoo photography, 170–171
  printed *versus* on-screen pictures, 10–11
  turning high-resolution images into Web-friendly
      images, 153–157
retail printing options, 164

RGB color model, defined, 189. *See also* Adobe RGB; sRGB

rotating images in Photoshop Elements, 134–135

S

Sample All Layers option, 45, 148

saturation
adjusting in Raw converter, 20
adjusting with Hue/Saturation filter, 119, 120–121, 168–169, 176
defined, 118, 189
dialing back, 118–119
increasing, 119, 168–169, 176
in printed colors, 119

Save for Web dialog box, 153–157

Save Optimized As dialog box, 157

saving
converted image options, 15, 22, 42, 149
cropped images, 141
in DNG format, 22
in PSD format, 15, 22, 42, 149
selection outlines, 42
separate grayscale images, 128
in TIFF format, 15, 22
which format to save in, 15, 22, 42, 149

scene modes
Action, 49, 51, 96, 171, 172, 193
defined, 49, 189
illustrated, 49, 193
Landscape, 50, 94, 95, 193
Nighttime, 193
Portrait, 49, 50, 57, 80, 162, 193
symbols, 49, 193

SD Card, defined, 189

selectable zone autofocus, 92, 189

selecting, 38–42, 189

Selection Brush tool
Add to Selection option, 39, 41
baboon image example, 175
Hardness value, 39–40, 41
lion statue example, 83
Mask mode, 38, 39, 83
Mode control, 38, 83
overview, 38
Selection mode, 41, 83
setting options, 38–39
Subtract from Selection option, 39, 41

selection outlines
applying Magic Wand tool in, 43–45
baboon image example, 175

defined, 38, 189
feathering, 175
illustrated, 41
lion statue example, 83
loading, 42
saving, 42

selection tools, defined, 38. *See also* Magic Wand tool; Rectangular Marquee tool; Selection Brush tool

self-timer, 88, 193

sepia-toned images, 129–130

shadows
adjusting by using Shadows/Highlights filter, 73–74, 167
adjusting in Raw converter, 19, 20

Shadows/Highlights filter
Darken Highlights slider, 74, 167
Lighten Shadows slider, 73, 167
Midtone Contrast slider, 74, 167

shaking, camera. *See* digital cameras, steadying

sharpening
defined, 102, 189
how it works, 102
in Raw converter, 21
refining, 105–106
role of Unsharp Mask filter, 102, 103–105
saving images, 107
when to use, 21

shift-tilt lenses, 136

shutter, 48, 189. *See also* shutter speed

shutter button, pressing, 51, 89, 92, 93

shutter lag, defined, 97

shutter-priority autoexposure
alternatives to, 96
applying EV compensation, 55, 160
defined, 49, 189
for freezing action, 96
switching to, 96
symbol, 96, 193
waterfall example, 98–99
zoo photography example, 171, 172

shutter speed
defined, 48, 49, 189
highest, invoking Action scene mode for, 51, 96
increasing to avoid blur, 87, 96–97
relationship to aperture, 48–49, 51, 80
setting, 49, 50–51
slow, when to use, 98–99
when to use tripod, 55, 87, 98, 181
zoo photography example, 171–172

Shutterfly, 164

slave flash, 65, 189

slow-synch flash, defined, 189

SLR lenses, digital, 100, 101, 111, 112
small RGB. *See* sRGB
SmartMedia, defined, 189
Snapfish, 164
spectrum. *See* gamut
Sports scene mode. *See* Action scene mode
spot metering
  defined, 52, 189
  versus pattern metering, 161
  symbol, 52, 193
  when to use, 53
sRGB
  versus Adobe RGB, 24–25
  as color management tool, 29, 197, 198
  defined, 189
  description, 24
stabilization. *See* image stabilization
stopping down the aperture, 94, 172, 180, 189
studio lights, 65, 67, 68
stylus. *See* pressure-sensitive tablets
Sunny symbol, 193
sunset images, 54, 62–63, 73, 166–169
symbols, 49, 52, 193

T

tablets, 34
tagged image file format. *See* TIFF format
temperature. *See* color temperature
tents, light, 67, 180
TIFF format
  creating JPEG copies, 179
  defined, 14, 189–190
  saving images in, 15, 22
  shooting pictures in, 15, 16
  when to use, 42, 149
tilted images, straightening, 134–135
Tolerance control, Magic Wand, 43–44
translucency, 33. *See also* opacity
tripods
  invoking self-timer mode, 88
  types, 87
  when to use, 55, 87, 98, 181
TWAIN driver, defined, 190

U

umbrellas, diffuser, 67, 68
Undo feature, 116, 148
Universal Serial Bus (USB), defined, 190

Unsharp Mask filter
  baboon image example, 175
  defined, 102, 190
  vintage train example, 102, 103–105
USB (Universal Serial Bus), defined, 190

V

vibration reduction, 87
viewfinder, camera
  versus camera monitor, 86
  checking focus, 101
  parallax errors, 27

W

warmer images, ways to create, 111, 112–113, 163, 164,
    192. *See also* white balance
warming filters, 112, 164, 190. *See also* Photo Filter tool
waterfall example, 98–99
WB. *See* white balance
Web-friendly images
  image quality *versus* file size, 156
  quick reference, 192
  turning high-resolution images into, 153–157
Web-safe colors, 37, 190
white balance
  adjusting camera, 59, 61, 110–111, 113, 164
  adjusting in Photoshop Elements, 19, 113
  defined, 190
  manual, 110–111
  quick reference, 192
  symbols, 113, 164, 193
white eye, repairing, 124–126
whole-frame metering, 193. *See also* pattern metering
wider-gamut color spaces, 24–25, 190. *See also*
    Adobe RGB
window, using to avoid using flash, 56–57, 58
Windows computers
  Adobe Gamma, 28, 29
  Camera Raw file extensions, 17
  color management options, 198, 199
  cursor options, 35
  monitor profiling, 28, 29
  on-screen photographs, 75
  Organizer, 13
World Wide Web
  specifying connection speed, 154
  turning high-resolution images into Web-friendly
    images, 153–157

X

xD-Picture Card, defined, 190

Y

yellow, 131. *See also* CMYK color model
yellow eye, repairing, 124–126

Z

zones, autofocus, 91–92, 93
zoo photography example, 170–176
zoom lenses
  versus digital zoom, 23, 81
  lion statue example, 80–81
  macro focusing options, 100
  product image example, 94–95
  rhino image example, 181
Zoom tool, 31